A SHORT HISTORY OF HOLMES BIBLE COLLEGE

A Greenville Miracle

He is Still Jehovah Jireh and More than Enough

Dr. Stan York

True Potential
REACH THE WORLD

All Scripture quotations, unless otherwise noted, are from the King James Version of the Bible.

A Brief History of Holmes Bible College: A Greenville Miracle

Cover and Interior Page design by True Potential, Inc.

ISBN: (Paperback): 9781960024169
ISBN: (e-book): 9781960024176
LCCN: 2023942673

True Potential

REACH THE WORLD

True Potential, Inc.
PO Box 904, Travelers Rest, SC 29690
www.truepotentialmedia.com
Produced and Printed in the United States of America.

Contents

Tribute to Jack and Jane Shaw

We honor and give a special thank you to Jack and Jane Shaw of Greenville, SC. This couple has provided the funds to create and print this first *History of Holmes Bible College.*

Jack attended Emmanuel College, Elon University, and Holmes Bible College. He has Honorary Doctorate Degrees from Anderson University and Regent University. He served a season as a teacher at Holmes Bible College.

Jack and Jane Shaw were instrumental in relocating Holmes Bible College to the present site. The land was obtained through their influence and gifts. The main campus is named the Leslie-Shaw Campus of Holmes Bible College. The campus is named after their parents—William Erby and Mittie Saxon Shaw (Jack) and Waldo and Angeline D. Leslie (Jane).

Jack is the founder, Chairman of the Board, and President of Shaw Resources, Inc., a residential and commercial real estate development and property management corporation that serves the Upstate, S.C., pockets of the low country, S.C. and North Carolina, and areas as far as the state of Oklahoma.

Jack and Jane have proven themselves to be effective and successful in business. They are dedicated civil servants and, most importantly, humble servants of Christ. They have built a legacy of faith and have lived lives of generosity and service. They have three children and seven grandchildren.

There are three things for sure. They love the Lord, each other (64 years married in August), AND Holmes Bible College.

We say, "Thank you!"

Sincerely,

D. Chris Thompson, President

Holmes Bible College

Introduction

History is replete with new beginnings covering every aspect of life. In the 1800s to the early 1900s in the religious world, ministers, both men and women, rediscovered the Wesleyan understanding of entire sanctification. Proponents from Phoebe Palmer and Sarah Lankford with their "Tuesday Meetings for the Promotion of Holiness," Timothy Merritt, Charles Finney and Asa Mahan with Oberlin College, Beverly Carradine, L. L. Pickett, Henry Clay Morrison, and A.B. Crumpler stormed the country preaching and teaching on the "Crisis Moment" in which one could experience the Holy Spirit reach deep into one's soul and experience the roots of sin being cut off. Phoebe Palmer taught the "Altar Theology" concerning Sanctification, or one only needs to ask for sanctification, and it is received. Also, many Holiness ministers and evangelists taught that the Sanctification experience was joined with the Baptism of the Holy Spirit.

The new Sanctification message led to the formation of the National Holiness Association from 1867-1894. Reverends John S. Inskip and William B. Osborn joined hands in establishing this Holiness Association. Holiness camp meetings began in Vineland, New Jersey, on July 17, 1867, and the following year these camp meetings spread throughout the Northeast, mostly on Methodist Campgrounds. After the Civil War, holiness meetings and the message found a home in the South as Holiness newspapers, magazines, and books spread the message. Nickels John Holmes and his wife, Lucy, eventually encountered the new message, and a spiritual hunger developed in their hearts for this experience.

John Wesley and these new holiness preachers used Ezekiel 36:25-29b English Standard Version (ESV);

> I will sprinkle clean water on you, and **you shall be clean from all your uncleannesses, and from all your idols I will cleanse you.** 26 <u>And I will give you a new heart, and a new spirit I will put within you. And I will remove the heart of stone from your flesh and give you a heart of flesh.</u> 27 **And I will put my Spirit within you, and cause you to walk in my statutes and be careful to obey my rules.** 28 You shall dwell in the land that I gave to your fathers, and you shall be my people, and I will be your God. 29 <u>And I will deliver you from all your uncleannesses.</u> (boldface and underline added by the author)

The Wesleyan teaching was not without challenges. Calvinist/Reformed theology taught sanctification began after one accepted salvation, including the idea that sanctification gradually continued until one's death or glorification. The Keswick and Northfield Conferences taught sanctification from this theological viewpoint. Later Holmes encountered these differences with his Presbyterian Synod, Christian and Missionary Alliance, and McClurkan's Pentecostal Mission.

Yet we may say that the Northfield Conference associated with D. L. Moody placed Holmes on the path to establishing a Bible or Christian training school. In the summer of 1893, he initiated the foundation for this school with Bible study among several people on Paris Mountain, South Carolina. From the first summer session to the twenty-first century, Holmes Bible College has been non-denominational, a faith school to train men and women as Gospel ministers by establishing churches or missionaries for the home missions or the foreign lands. This history seeks to provide insight into the persons and places and, most importantly, allow the voices of Holmes students, supporters, and professors to witness the Divine direction in establishing Holmes Bible College. Listen closely to these voices as you will witness life changes for God's glory and workers entering the harvest fields.

We will look at the context of Greenville County and the South. It is important to understand any obstacles that challenged the school's formation in the Post-Reconstruction Era. A brief biography of Holmes invites us to look at informative life events leading to God's Call on his life as a lawyer and pastor. His biography introduces many leading Holiness/Pentecostal pastors and denominations. These facts aid in establishing a theological foundation for the school. The school moved from Paris Mountain to Atlanta, Georgia to Columbia, South Carolina, and eventually it returned to Paris Mountain. Finally, Paris Mountain relocated to Briggs Avenue as the student body grew. A new campus resides in Travelers Rest, South Carolina. Allow the story of the world's oldest Pentecostal Bible School to provide eyes, hearts, and a vision for your future ministry.

1. The Family

The world of Southern living in 1847 was an agrarian culture. The phrase "Cotton is King" provided the establishment of the economic culture that pervaded the South. Cotton economics created many problematic issues, mainly the morality and ethics of slavery during the Pre and Post Civil War days. This was the atmosphere into which Nickels John Holmes was born. Studying the culture establishes a context for understanding the actions and reactions in one's life.

His father, Zelotes Lee Holmes, originally from New York State, was born on January 3, 1815. Zelotes' father died when he was three years old, and his mother nine years later. An older brother assumed responsibility for Zelotes until he reached age seventeen. Later, Zelotes made a decision to help his brother by taking on the responsibility for his education and living. His early education was in a classical academy in Buffalo, New York. Eventually, he moved to Meadville, Pennsylvania, to attend Allegheny College. After two years, he left school due to his health and money issues. Eventually, Zelotes traveled to St. Louis for work. Once again, his work ended. With little money, he needed to decide whether to return to Buffalo or go elsewhere.

Zelotes took a steamer boat trip from St. Louis to Knoxville, Tennessee, as his funds were insufficient to continue his journey. He worked in Knoxville, until he saved sufficient funds to continue to Columbia, South Carolina. In 1839 he began attending a Presbyterian Seminary. He received a stipend from an education society and accepted a job teaching mathematics at a local female seminary for his financial support. Zelotes' persistence led to graduating from Columbia Seminary in 1842.

After his graduation, he was licensed in 1842 in the Presbyterian Church. His first assignment was Nazareth Presbyterian Church in Spartanburg. He received his ordination orders in April 1843. One year later, he married Miss Kate Nickels of Laurens County. The couple would have twelve children, with only seven surviving to adulthood. Nickels John Holmes was born on September 9, 1847. He was the oldest son of the family. In 1849, Reverend Holmes left the Nazareth Church and took residence in Laurens County.

Zelotes' pastoral ministry led him to serve several churches in the Laurens County area. Along with serving various churches, he was elected State Clerk of the Presbytery. As a salary supplement, he became a professor for Laurensville Female College; then later, he accepted a professorship at the College of Clinton, which eventually became Presbyterian College.[1]

Early Childhood of N. J. Holmes

The formative years of one's life provide insight into the life and mission of a child; Nick Holmes[2] was no exception. This mischievous young child was shaped by Godly parents. Holmes wrote, "My father was a real Presbyterian preacher and believed that children should be taught to do right, corrected when wrong, and memorize the Shorter Catechism." He described his mother as "an earnest, pious Christian woman, who loved her children, and took to heart the exhortations of Solomon concerning child raising."[3] The religious instruction was taught lovingly with the goal of raising obedient, honorable children.

Nick was never considered a studious lad in his younger years. School, for him, was more a distraction from his desire to maintain his free spirit. Even as a twelve-year-old attending Laurens Academy, he was more concerned with maintaining a tough image that led to several fights with his classmates. He was given a gun and hunting dogs, so the woods lured him many times into foolish actions. As his grades declined, his father took away his dogs in hopes of Nick refocusing his talents on education. Being a wise man, he finally decided to put his son's hand to the plow as a remedy to reorient his focus. Removed from school, farm work provided the discipline to gain Nick's attention and ready him for school.[4]

There are three critical events in his life that require attention. It is important to study these events to understand the future character development of Nick Holmes. Possibly Holmes' words provided insight:

I was not a Christian at this time. I had this temper but was never a quarrelsome boy nor hard to get along with, and it was not often I had difficulties with others. I never learned to use profane or vulgar language. My mother drilled it into my mind and heart from the earliest youth that it was wrong.[5]

The first event occurred during the construction of the Octagon House for his family in Laurens. Nick was fourteen years old. His parents had traveled away from home. He wanted to use the carpenter's saw and was denied its use. After arguing with the carpenter, Nick grabbed a hatchet and attempted to throw it at the carpenter. In Holmes' words, he described this event:

Somehow just as my hand was coming around with the hatchet, some mysterious impulse or power like a flash of lightning checked me, and I gripped the hatchet fast and held it back, and it came down on the work bench very near him and cut a hole in his hat.[6]

The second event happened one day as I took a stick and began to hit a friend for no specific reason. In the midst of my anger my friend cried out, "Why are you beating me?" In a moment in a twinkling of an eye, something may spring up before us that may revolutionize our whole life. An enemy may spring out to thwart our pathway or a friend may rise up to help us on the way. Let us watch and be ready. We know not what shall be.[7]

The last event was early during the Civil War when he was roughly fifteen years old. Salt was a scarce commodity, and his father sent him to the north of Georgetown to make salt. One morning during their work, he desired to ride from camp. He argued with a wagon driver over the use of a bridle. Upon refusing to receive one, his anger grew, and he threatened to shoot the man. Nick went to his tent and retrieved his gun. Mr. Hampton, the overseer, saw him with the gun and stopped him. Recalling this event, he wrote:

I was of course very sorry that I had been so angry and so foolish. It gave me another occasion to be ashamed of myself, and to thank God that He save me again from the shedding of blood.[8]

Looking into Holmes' future, these three events opened the door for providing a witness to the Atonement's power to sanctify a person from anger.

He wrote:

> I doubly thank God that through His abounding grace the evil principle within me has been crucified with Christ—put to death, and that the love of God has filled the place in my being. Now I have no more need, thank God, for carnal weapons.[9]

Holmes' father used to take him to revival meetings around Laurens. In 1863 while attending a service with his father in Clinton, Holmes made a commitment to Christ. He records. "But I remember that with tears and sorrow for my sins I confessed and professed faith in Christ, and took a definite stand for Christ."[10] He joined the church and witnessed to others about salvation through Christ. His older sister Olive became sick, and before her death, she said to Nick, "You are to preach the gospel."[11] These words struck him deeply. In the future, these words rang as a bell in his heart.

War Service and University Years

The War Between The States was changing the landscape of the South as Holmes was seventeen; he wanted to join the army. Given permission to join, he joined a group that was chosen to guard a Union prison camp in Florence, SC. The message from Olive resounded in his heart "Preach the Gospel." He attempted to drown these words with his duties at the prison. One more event occurred to change his life.

He was selected to guard a train traveling to Wilmington, NC. He was told to allow no women on the train. At the Florence stop, he saw a woman in a black dress wearing a veil. She requested permission for a ride with them. Holmes repeated to the woman his orders to allow no women on board. This mother's appeal touched his heart. Her son was wounded, and she needed to see him. Holmes repeated his orders several times, then allowed the mother aboard. The significance of this event reveals a changed heart in the angry young man. Yes, he disobeyed his orders, but he developed compassion for folks in distress.[12]

Post-Civil War years in the South were times of depression, worthless money, limited goods such as cotton for sale, starvation, and educational systems destroyed or suspended. Nick was roughly eighteen years old upon his return home. His father chose Scotland as Nick's education destination and enrolled him at the University of Edinburgh. Tuition payment came from assembling a few bales of cotton for sale in Liverpool, England. The cotton broker in Liverpool failed and lost the cotton money for education and personal expenses. Due to his early dislike of education and service in the Confederate Army, Holmes found himself behind in his studies.

Nick spent three years studying at the University of Edinburgh. Spring 1867 found Holmes going to Paris, where he met with his Uncle Simpson and family. There they attended the 1867 World's Exposition. After this occasion, Holmes and his cousin left for Germany. Their goal was to study and learn the German language. Confronted with the differences in culture, such as drinking, horse racing, and other activities, he observed the culture critically. Upon his return to Scotland, he began his second term at Edinburgh. This was a time of intense study and preparation for examinations in the third year.[13] During his third year, he traveled throughout the countryside of Scotland. As he read and studied for examinations and his return home in the spring of 1869, he confessed that the ring of "Preach the Gospel" rang clearly in his ears and heart.[14] As he considered the various allurements from France and Germany, he wrestled with his future calling. He wrote, "The thought in my mind was a compromised life. I wanted to work for God, but I did not want to be a preacher ordained and set apart to preach the Gospel."[15] Upon his return, he discovered compromise was not possible.

Lawyer Years and Ministry Call

Nick quickly learned all his efforts were futile as he attempted to farm and teach school. Finally, he studied law. In 1870 he passed his bar examinations and was admitted to practice law. He formed a partnership with W. Y. Simpson and practiced together until Mr. Simpson was elected governor of South Carolina. Eventually, Governor Simpson became Chief Justice of the Supreme Court, and the Simpson Law Firm became the young lawyer's work.[16]

Nick married Miss Lucy Elizabeth Simpson on February 29, 1876; she was W. D. Simpson's daughter. Holmes practiced law for fourteen years. The new law partnership was very successful, yet he could never escape the words of his sister Olive. Being very established in law practice, he decided to run for the Office of Solicitor in his judicial circuit. Then he heard the Holy Spirit speak clearly on the Courthouse steps in Laurens County, "You are seeking an office to prosecute men for crime. Had you not better seek to save them from the commission of crime?"[17] This prompting led him to abandon seeking the solicitor position. Suddenly he could not read law. His desire to meet with clients waned, and he reached a decision point. He approached his wife with the question of entering the ministry, and she responded, "Do as you feel led, and what God would have you do."[18] Holmes sought the advice of two pastors concerning the call. Baptist Pastor J. D. Pitts advised him, "I do not believe you will ever be satisfied until you preach."[19] Finally, a Presbyterian pastor encouraged him to consult the Presbytery and provide a statement of facts, then allow them to decide the issue of his ministry call. He continued seeking guidance from others as he sought to fulfill the ministerial call. He wrote his father-in-law, W. D. Simpson, seeking advice and received this response, "But at last you must seek counsel from a higher power, do what your own good sense may determine.... There certainly is no higher or more sacred calling than the ministry."[20] Finally, he learned about the next meeting of the Presbytery and traveled to address his calling. He wrote his mother about this meeting to seek licensing, and she wrote him. "She said to someone that she had prayed for forty years that one of her sons might preach the Gospel...she had given up all hope, when I decided to preach."[21]

He attended the Presbytery Meeting and gave his testimony concerning the ministry call to preach. He was approved for a preaching license without a Seminary requirement. His first work began in Spartanburg as a pulpit replacement for Rev. R. F. Wilson. At the next Presbytery, he received ordination as a Presbyterian Evangelist with a salary of a thousand dollars. As an evangelist, he received confirmation in his call and established six or eight churches in the Presbytery of Enoree.[22] These initial ministry years revealed fruit for his labors, yet deep inside, Holmes discerned a struggle for a deeper life in Christ.

2. Founding Holmes Bible College

Evangelistic Work, Northfield Conference, and Sanctification

The early evangelistic days for Holmes provided occasions for praise and deep concern for his ministry. The spiritual conditions discovered among churches mirrored struggles as the southern states rebuilt after the Civil War. Many questions faced southern folk during these years, such as rebuilding the economy from a major dependence upon cotton, the demands of the Reconstruction Period upon folks for property redistribution, new state constitutions, adjusting farms to limited manpower due to slavery's abolishment, occupation of Northern troops to enforce Reconstruction programs, "Lost Cause" ideology, and the rise of terror from the Ku Klux Klan and Knights of the White Camellia.

Holmes wrote, "In the Presbytery...we found a great lack of spiritual life and power."[23]

The resounding message in Holmes' ear was, "Preach the Gospel!" In his work among the Presbyterian churches, he discovered:

> Sinners converted and started the Christian life, believers realized that they were not doing much for God or living as they ought to. They would try to consecrate and reconsecrate, and do better and live better, but they found it a hard struggle, and we did too....[24]

Then he found D. L. Moody's book, *The Secret of Power*, and N. J. and Lucy discovered new insights into the Holy Spirit's work. This book reading generated a hunger for the Holy Spirit in their lives. What is revealed in this discovery was a tension between Reformed and Wesleyan theology over the work of Sanctification and the Holy Spirit. Reformed theology taught 'cessation' of the gifts of the Holy Spirit; that they were given for the founding of the Church only. Sanctification was gained upon regeneration and a gradual work until glorification or death, versus the Reformed accusation of Wesleyans teach that they do not sin. Thus, a tension developed among the Reformed faith folks during the late 1800s as the Holiness message was proclaimed by Wesleyan evangelists. The tension resided in the Wesleyan teaching that Sanctification was received during a 'crisis moment' plus the misunderstanding of Christian Perfection wasn't 'static perfection' (sinlessness) but 'being perfected in love.'[25]

Soon after N. J. learned about Moody's Northfield Bible Conference held every July, he developed a hunger for greater insight into the work of the Holy Spirit.[26] Herein lies Holmes' tension with a seemingly unfruitful ministry or the tension between Reformed and Wesleyan teaching. At this point, I must inject the uneasiness of Holmes that was being discovered and felt among many Presbyterians. Again he addressed this issue.

> This was not as we had learned it, and I opposed it and preached against it, but at the same time, I was not satisfied with my own experience, and thought sometimes that my life was more theory than a real experience...I became more and more anxious to know more about the Holy Spirit and His work.[27]

Under the conviction of the Holy Spirit, he began to recall the lack of power in his ministry, the work of Presbyterian ministers, and the church membership. As Holmes prayed and ministered, he confessed eventually:

> I saw from reading that little book what I had not seen from reading books on Theology. That there is a remedy and that we did not have to pass on without it. That difficulty was opened up in the work of the Holy Ghost.[28]

The spiritual hunger led N. J. and Lucy Holmes to attend the Northfield Bible Conference in Northfield, Massachusetts during the summer of 1891. They attended two conferences, one for students, and the General Conference for Christian workers. The Holmes spent time in prayer and seeking Scriptures to teach them about the Holy Spirit. Also, N. J. had a strong desire to meet and counsel with Moody. One afternoon his desire was fulfilled as Moody visited the cottage rented by the Holmes and took N. J. for a buggy ride. This encounter stirred a crisis moment for Holmes. Moody shared that the experience of the Deeper Life begins with a humble vessel for the Holy Spirit's filling. During this ride, Moody stopped the buggy and told Holmes to remove his hat for prayer. Holmes recalled this moment, "He seemed to pray right up to heaven for me, and I felt very much blessed and helped by his conversation and prayer."[29]

N. J. and Lucy attended the next conference and received teaching from F. B. Meyer, A. J. Gordon, and other Deeper Life teachers. These meetings stirred the Holmes couple to intense study and prayer for God to reveal Himself in new ways for their ministry. So deeply were these meetings upon them, "We could see it and feel it down in our hearts. We soon saw that it would not do throw ourselves back into human creeds, and cold systems of Theology."[30] The messages were filled with a call for total consecration for God's work in His servants, so His Work reached the ears and hearts of the hearers. Holmes recalled the speakers made no difference between Sanctification and the Baptism of the Holy Spirit. He wrote:

Rev. N.J. and Lucy S. Holmes

In fact they did not emphasize sanctification much, or consider it necessary as a preparation for the baptism with the Holy Ghost. I sought as I thought earnestly for the experience, as set forth by Mr. F. B. Meyer, who was a blessed man and teacher, but I failed in some way to surrender. I had so much more to surrender than I had any idea of at first. I had never apprehended the crucifixion of the old man, and I found many of the works of flesh still hanging about me, and even coming out from my heart.[31]

This was the beginning of Holmes' struggle with Reformed teaching over Sanctification and the Baptism of the Holy Spirit. One fleshly issue was fear for his ministerial credentials, church members, and peoples' opinions. Yet he continued the search for this deeper life. His wife, Lucy, received a blessed experience which we called the baptism with the Holy Ghost under the teaching there.[32] Lucy's experience came over her as she repented of all dead works, and her inner spirit was consumed with Divine Love.

Upon return from the Northfield Conference, the Holmes were consumed with a new vision and hunger for evangelism. Now Lucy became an integral part of their ministry. Before her Northfield experience, she was a shy, quiet witness for the Gospel, now N. J. recalled:

> God blessed us in the unity of our experience and conceptions of the Bible truths, and we rejoiced to see the light and abounding life of Christ flash in other hearts, and see their faces beam with divine love, and see them walk in the sanctified way.[33]

In 1891 the Presbytery called upon N. J. to form a second Presbyterian congregation in Greenville, South Carolina. Even as he felt evangelism work as his call, he submitted to the Presbytery. The folks soon called Holmes to remain as their minister. This was his first and only pastorate as a Presbyterian minister. Submitting to God's will as a pastor became an important revelation for Holmes as this preparation empowered his future evangelistic meetings and introduction of Deeper Life ministry.

In 1894 Holmes became restless to return to the evangelistic field. His departure from the Second Church was not due to any disagreements but solely as yielding to God for a new ministry. In the fall of 1895, he was released from the pastorate to general evangelistic work within the bounds of the Synod of South Carolina with a salary of fifteen hundred dollars.[34] This restlessness within his heart was a stirring from the Northfield Conference to preach a Deeper Life. He wrote, "He was revealing to me the truth of the Bible, on the subject of sanctification, holiness, divine healing, and the work of the Spirit in a new light."[35] Now Holmes began to understand the call and meaning of "Preach the Gospel" as spoken by his sister Olive.

1895 became a critical year for Holmes and his ministry. While preaching at Gray Court, Laurens County, South Carolina, for Reverend J. W. Shell, the Holy Spirit confronted him. The new emphasis on a Deeper Life with God was shared with all people in the evangelistic meetings. One night while closing the service, Holmes heard the Holy Spirit speak to him:

You have told others what to do. Have you done it yourself? I said, no Lord, I have not, but I will do it today. And though I had been struggling over the question for over two years, I did not dare to let it go over that day. So that evening before the sun went down, I went into an old barn…and I began to talk to God, as if the question of my complete yielding and surrender to Him must be settled then and there….[36]

This memorable day was July 7, 1895. This was the first of three experiences of the Holy Spirit's confirmation of Sanctification in his life. Holmes recalled during prayer a:

…flash of power that went through my body like an electric current, and passed away, and then there was a wonderful peace that came into my heart, like the peace that passeth all understanding. I felt that all was at rest in God, and that I was indeed His to do His will.[37]

Again the Holy Spirit visited him at Mountville in April 1896. While praying in the woods, he felt his heart burn within. Later on May 28, 1896, in Bamberg, while praying after reading Andrew Murray's, *Christ Our Life*, God's presence burned with him until he rejoiced aloud in an ecstasy of joy and love.[38] These experiences witnessed by Holmes are repeated in numerous life stories of Holiness evangelists. John Wesley recalled his heart burned within him; the result of this encounter was the Wesleyan Revival in England for fifty-plus years. With the confirmation of Sanctification, Holmes now stood at a new chapter in his life.

Identity

The growth of the Holiness Movement spread nationwide between the 1850s and the early 1900s. As holiness evangelists like Beverly Carradine, Henry Clay Morrison, A. B. Crumpler, G. D. Watson, Asa Mahan, Charles Finney, John S. Inskip, Catherine Booth, Benjamin T. Roberts, Seth Rees, A. B. Simpson, Daniel Warner, and many others traversed the United States preaching Holiness in churches, tent meetings, and national Holiness Camp Meetings, the need for teachers, evangelists, preachers, and missionaries grew. This Wesleyan Revival needed messengers to spread the Sanctification message, thus sparking a new generation of Bible Schools, Colleges, and Institutes. Even the Reformed theological ministers such as Charles Finney and Asa Mahan, founders of Oberlin theology or a blend of Presbyterian/ Methodist holiness understanding, who had accepted the Sanctification message needed teaching and training such as the Chicago Evangelization Society in 1886 eventually becoming Moody Bible Institute. A sample list of Holiness schools includes Houghton Seminary, later Houghton College 1883 (Wesleyan), Seattle Seminary later Seattle Pacific College 1891 (Free Methodist), Asbury College 1890 (Methodist & other Wesleyan denominations), 1900 God's Bible School (non-denominational), 1907 Toccoa Falls College (Alliance), 1882 Nyack College (Alliance) and 1911 Trevecca College later Trevecca Nazarene College (Nazarene).

Holmes wrote:

> For many years the thought of some kind of a Bible or Christian training school, for Christian workers had been on my mind and heart…Long before we purchased the mountain we would travel in our work, my mind and eyes were on the lookout for a suitable place for a Bible School.[39]

One might assume this vision was birthed with his Northfield Conference experience, yet his evangelistic meetings around the Laurens and Spartanburg area weighed more on this decision.

The Sanctification experience for Holmes empowered his preaching as never before. His calls to the lost for salvation, sanctification, or healing strengthened the ministry among the Presbyterian churches plus created theological tensions with the South Carolina Presbytery. Holiness preaching and teaching generated similar tensions among the Methodist Episcopal Church South (MECS). Even though the Holiness message echoed John Wesley's ministry in England and the early days of Methodism in the colonies, early Holiness evangelists stirred congregations throughout the South by raising the question concerning "Was this new message among Methodists true to their doctrine?" A. B. Crumpler, a Holiness Methodist evangelist in North Carolina, was brought to trial by the Methodists as they used Rule 301 to charge him over holiness preaching.

Rule 301 was adopted in 1894 at the Methodist Episcopal Church South General Conference as the issue of traveling holiness evangelists became an issue for many pastors. Holiness preachers in the Gainesville District of Georgia had changed names on churches to "Holiness Churches." Bishop Atticus Haygood led the anti-holiness clergy to stop these actions by Holiness evangelists. Rule 301 forbade evangelists to conduct meetings in the bounds of a Methodist charge without the pastor's consent.[40] Bishop Haygood and his anti-holiness supporters now used the Book of Discipline to control the traveling evangelists. Vinson Synan wrote:

> After this statement, it was clear that the Holiness Crusade had gained strength since the founding of the National Holiness Association in 1867 had failed to call Methodism back to the Holiness message of its founder, and that the future effective proclamation of the doctrine would of necessity be outside the bounds of Methodism. This was the climax and crisis that signaled an exodus from the church and the beginning of numerous Holiness sects that appeared throughout the nation after 1894.[41]

The Presbyterian Church of South Carolina heard rumblings about a teaching different from their theological positions on sanctification, divine healing, and the Holy Spirit. Holmes became troubled by these concerns and approached his Synod. He wrote, "I went to the committee that had the work in charge, and told them about my views, and I did not want them to be embarrassed by my position, and that I would resign." The chairman and committee expressed a desire for Holmes to continue his work. After this meeting, Holmes' cousin, Ernest, wrote to him on November 8, 1897:

> Your letter received and it was greatly welcomed. Very glad the difficulty in Presbytery has been reconciled or settled and that Cousin Nick and others will not leave the Presbyterian Church. Nick is such a tower of strength that Presbyterianism would receive a heavy blow by his departure from the Church and all Presbytery.[42]

The Southern Presbytery of Louisville, Kentucky, held a trial for Reverend M. H. Houston, a future Altamont teacher, in 1897. The Cincinnati Enquirer reported on this inquiry on September 9, 1897. The article, ALL THE WAY, reported Dr. M. H. Houston was recalled from China for:

> ...deviating from the articles of the church's faith in his teachings. Dr. Houston made a vigorous defense and delivered a ringing speech. "He differs in his views from the standards of the church. He holds

to a sort of sanctification, but says he does not believe in sinless perfection...and he believes that under certain circumstances women may speak in public in exposition of the Scriptures."[43]

Houston's final fate rested in the National General Assembly.

Houston addressed his views with a strong defense. He said:

> The Westminster Standards, which are the confessional symbols of the Presbyterian Church, are rich in scriptural truth. But they were written two hundred and fifty years ago, when the life of the church, in some respects, was not developed as it is now. In common, therefore, with other confessional symbols of that time, they are defective in their assessment of the doctrine of sanctification, the truth which concerns most intimately the life of the Christian.[44]

The final decision was given on December 15, 1897. The Louisville Courier-Journal reported the final findings of the National General Assembly. Dr. Houston was allowed a final defense of his views; the final vote was cast during an evening session with a vote of 10-3 for censure. The Judiciary Committee was ordered to prepare the articles of censure and to formulate a proper judgment for presentation on December 16.[45] On December 20, Houston was found guilty of heresy preaching the doctrine of sanctification. The Burlingame Enterprise reported, "A majority favored his expulsion, but the majority decided that he should be admonished to cease talking or suffer suspension."[46] Houston surrendered his orders on December 23. He wrote,:

> I now give back to the Presbytery of Louisville all rights and privileges that I received in my ordination as a minister of the Presbyterian Church, and I take my place as a private member of the Church...With earnest prayer to Him in behalf of all the members of the Presbytery, I remain, no longer your co-presbyter, but always your friend and servant in Christ.[47]

Dr. Houston continued his membership in the Presbyterian Church as he later settled in Waynesboro, Virginia.

A year before Houston's resignation, Holmes decided to surrender his orders to the South Carolina Presbytery. This decision was hastened by Reverend S. C. Todd and Holmes due to the issue of their preaching sanctification, divine healing, and the Holy Spirit. Holmes wrote, "for the sake of peace to withdraw from the Presbytery which we agreed to do letters of discussion being granted us by the Presbytery."[48] Holmes united with the Brewerton Independent Presbyterian Church in 1896 as their views on sanctification and healing were like ours. The Brewerton Presbyterian Church left the South Carolina Presbytery in May 1899. Upon their departure, the members called Holmes to become their pastor. As reported in the *Anderson Intelligencer*, "The Brewerton church has sent a petition to presbytery asking to be allowed to withdraw on account of the congregation and a committee has been sent to investigate the case."[49] The newspaper article confirmed the organizing of Altamont Missionary and Bible Institute, but they called it Paris Mountain Bible Institute.[50] Holmes was very well known in Laurens County and founded several other churches during his evangelist travels with the South Carolina Presbytery. The newspaper continued:

> It is said that it is liot (sic) unlikely that some churches will follow the lead of the Brewerton church and cut loose from the Presbytery, endorse the Rev. Mr. Holmes' views and become independent organizations. Those opposed to Mr. Holmes say there is no foundation for this report.[51]

Now Holmes' vision of a Bible school becomes clearer.

Holmes, S. C. Todd, and M. H. Houston were released from their Presbyterian orders, then began to explore a relationship with other churches.

The Holiness movement created tension within denominations over the sanctification teaching. The Baptists in the Cape Fear District of North Carolina also experienced similar actions. Eventually, the Holiness preachers and folks separated to form their own Holiness Association and added to the Twelve Articles of Faith, a Thirteenth Article stating Sanctification as a "crisis event."

Identity is a crucial part of ministerial life. It opens the door for one's relationship with folks of a kindred spirit. The new message of the Holiness Movement sent Holmes, S. C. Todd, M. H. Houston, J. A. Culbreth, and J. M. Pike on a journey for association with kindred holiness spirits. This identity would aid in shaping Holmes' vision of a Bible training school for young men and women for ministry.

The issue of identity raised its ugly head as current and former Presbyterian pastors faced threats of rescinding ordination orders, placing pastors on trial for preaching holiness and sanctification, and creating tensions among various Presbyteries. The root of the controversy was Armenian/Wesleyan theology, and teaching sanctification was experienced in a 'crisis moment.' Accusations abounded from various Presbyterian trials; these were teaching holiness, sanctification, and healing. At risk for these Presbyterians were ministers who had experienced sanctification and brought this message to struggling churches. The doctrinal issue of predestination faced a challenge concerning Free Will. Yet a question remains to be answered, what movements, revivals, or ministers created the atmosphere of tension in the Presbyterian Church?

A critical look locates the Presbyterian quandary in the revivals of Gasper River and the preaching of James McGready, the Cane Ridge Revival, and the revival in the Cumberland region in southern Kentucky. The manifestations of shouting, rolling, fainting (slain in the Spirit), laughter, hollering, and barking challenged Presbyterian orthodoxy. Once again observe, several of these manifestations occurred during the Great Awakening under the preaching of Jonathan Edwards, George Whitefield, and the Tennants. The outcome was a division between Old Lights and New Lights. The Old Light/New Light reappeared in the challenges to Presbyterian Orthodoxy in Kentucky. The Washington Presbyterian of Ohio established the Synod of Kentucky on September 6, 1803.[52]

The trial of Reverend Richard McNemar by the Synod of Kentucky created an atmosphere of dissenters among the ministers' committee that eventually led to the creation of new synods for the New Lights. The dissenters insisted that in the final analysis, the Bible—not the Confession of Faith—was the criterion for the determination of theological legitimacy.[53] Barton Stone, the founder of the Christian Church (Disciples of Christ), was among the dissenters. He challenged the predestination position by teaching man was in a miserable state outside of God, yet believed he possessed "rational faculties, capable of knowing and enjoying God...faith was sufficient to achieve salvation was made possible by God."[54] The dissenters (revivalists) eventually formed two new synods, Springfield and Cumberland. Herein lies the contention between Old Lights and New Lights. The Cumberland Synod adopted in 1816 a confession of faith and a discipline. The new discipline relaxed educational requirements, emphasized a zealous commitment to evangelism, and softened of the Calvinist notion of election.[55] With trials, charges, and challenges to confessional theology, the Presbyterian Church in Kentucky grew more rigid and illiberal.[56]

These early Presbyterian battles shed light upon Holmes and Todd surrendering their credentials to the South Carolina Synod and M. H. Houston's ordination orders. The preaching of sanctification, healing in the Atonement, and the second coming of Christ stood outside the Confessional theology of the Presbyterians. How? As the Holiness message moved throughout the South, the issue of Free Will versus Predestination created denominational problems. Holmes solved his predicament with his affiliation to Brewerton Independent Presbyterian Church. Eventually, he and Reverend S. C. Todd found a kindred spirit with the Christian and Missionary Alliance. Todd became the Superintendent of the Southern Convention. Remember, Holmes preached once a month for the Brewerton church and did evangelistic work in South Carolina for his remaining month.

The Christian and Missionary Alliance principles attracted Holmes. These principles were 1) the CMA organized believers into small groups as "branches," and 2) the Fourfold Gospel of Jesus as Savior, Jesus as Sanctifier, Jesus as Healer, and Jesus as Soon Coming King, and affiliation with the CMA was a simple pledge to support these founding principles.[57] An additional issue for Holmes generated an agreement with Simpson over predestination. Simpson gave his testimony at the 1885 International Convention on Holiness and Divine Healing. He said, "Some twenty-seven years ago, I floundered for ten months in the waters of despondency, and I got out of there just by believing in Jesus as my Savior." Simpson was influenced by Walter Marshall's *Gospel Mystery of Sanctification* as he read, "The first good work you will ever perform is to believe on the Lord Jesus Christ."[58] Holmes' relationship with the CMA birthed another vision for a school for missionary training.

Holmes departed from the CMA during the Atlanta days of the Altamont Missionary and Bible Institute. Then he united with J. O. McClurkan of the Pentecostal Mission. Holmes never provided a reason for his departure.

McClurkan received his sanctification under the ministry of the Methodist evangelist Beverly Carradine in California in 1895. After his experience, McClurkan was scheduled for a year Sabbatical, and due to his sanctification experience, McClurkan took two years crossing the United States to return to his home in Nashville, Tennessee. McClurkan was a committed Calvinist doctrinally and worked out his Wesleyan message of Sanctification to function in his home of Cumberland Presbyterian Church.

N. J. Holmes joined another non-denominational group, the Pentecostal Mission, and received ordination in 1901 as a minister. Lucy Holmes was licensed as an Evangelist in 1901.[59]

One must ask this question, "How did Holmes' affiliation with the CMA and Pentecostal Mission define his future vision for ministry?" First, Holmes' call to evangelism was confirmed. The holiness message must be preached, and more workers became a necessity for this work. Secondly, folks hungered for solid Biblical teaching to walk with holiness, purity, and purpose. Capable Bible teachers were needed to fill this need. Thirdly, the mission fields aboard and at home begged for more to gather in the harvest of lost souls, and lastly, Holmes never lost his vision for female preachers and teachers. Remember, Lucy was licensed as an Evangelist in the Pentecostal Mission in 1901. With these goals in mind, Holmes set about to establish a Holiness Bible School and fulfill a burning desire in his heart.

Birth and Fulfillment of a Vision for the Bible School

> And the Lord answered me: "**Write the vision**; make it plain upon tablets, so he may run who reads it. [3] For still the vision awaits its time; it hastens to the end—it will not lie. **If it seem slow, wait for it; it will surely come, it will not delay.**[60] Habakkuk 2:2-3 RSV

These verses in Habakkuk resonate with the birth of the Altamont Missionary and Bible Institute (later Holmes Bible College). The term vision is from the Hebrew term, meaning a sight (mentally), such as: a dream, revelation, or oracle.

The earliest vision or impression of the Bible School belongs to Catherine Nickels, N. J.'s mother. A year before her death, she wrote to her son:

> I wanted a house of my own, and I wanted it filled with young people that I could train to serve the Lord. And when I married, as your father was a minister, I thought I could carry out my plan, but found out the Lord was not ready for the plan....[61]

God births visions or dreams in folks who are deeply desirous to walk with Him. A vision, at times, begins with a birth and excitement, then suddenly as it appears, the vision dies. The fulfillment of a vision occurs in *kairos* time (the Lord's timing). Catherine had a large family, yet it was her oldest son, Nickels John, who became the heir of this vision. Later she wrote:

> One day while at his house, my mind ran back over my life and his, and something said to me, "Your son shall carry out your plans." Now it has been fulfilled. My plan has been carried out. Praise the Lord![62]

During Holmes' Presbyterian evangelistic tours in South Carolina, he searched for a location to establish a Bible school. He wrote, "For many years the thought of some kind of a Bible or Christian training school for Christian workers had been on my mind and heart."[63] As did many folks capable of spending vacation time in the mountains to escape the Southern summer heat, N. J. and Lucy rented a small cottage on Paris Mountain for part of the summer in 1892. They enjoyed this area, purchased a few acres, and built a cottage.[64] Little did Holmes realize the original vision of his mother, Catherine, was taking form in founding the school. In 1893 the Holmes held their first summer Bible training session on Paris Mountain. For ten days to two weeks, young men listened attentively to Reverend Holmes teach the Word and pray. A tent was the housing erected on the property. The following summer, Holmes and his students erected a small Chapel for study and prayer.[65] These small beginnings of investing in Scriptural study with men eventually shaped the foundation for the Bible Institute. In 1898 Holmes, Todd, and others had the opportunity to purchase the Altamont Hotel on the highest point on Paris Mountain for the sum of five thousand dollars.[66] On August 30, 1898, Holmes began to divide his property holdings and wished "Mrs. Lutie Wright to have my part of the farm owned by my mother...I want my house and place which were (?) my fathers to be sold (?) for $1000.00 and given to the Bible and housing school on Paris Mountain."[67] Eventually, the other investors stopped their investment, and Holmes paid the difference owed on the Altamont Hotel. He and Lucy repaid the investors totally. Clarity of vision broke forth for N. J. and Lucy as his mother's vision became a reality.

On November 1, 1898, The Altamont Bible Institute opened on Paris Mountain in Greenville County, South Carolina. Law Anderson was the first student of the school. Dr. M. H. Houston, as earlier discussed, was the Bible teacher. As the month progressed, other students joined the school. Among those first students was Ella Brown from Turkey, North Carolina.[68] Eventually, the student body would increase from fifty to seventy students. In Law Anderson's history of Altamont, he recorded the winter of 1898 and 1899 as one of the severest winters the South had known for many years.[69] Several issues arose during the first year of school a shortage of firewood. During the Christmas days, the students had to cut and haul wood to warm the former hotel. Also, the water pipe from the water storage tank froze and required two men to climb to the top and lower buckets of water by rope to those below. Amazingly Anderson records, "There was no murmuring, complaining, or shrinking under the fire of the trials, but everyone kept sweet, happy, and joyous all the time. They all believed that Rom. 8:28 was a living truth."[70]

The teachers during the first term of the Institute were M. H. Houston for the Pentateuch, Matthew, Acts, Romans, and Revelation; Miss Lucy Jones of London, Kentucky, for English; Miss Nellie Hackney for music.[71] Rev. Holmes maintained his evangelistic meetings most of the time. The second term began on April 1, 1899, with its completion on October 1. Anderson wrote that God manifested his love and power in healing sick bodies during this term.[72]

The teachers worked without a salary and ate at the same table as the students. Holmes wrote:

> The whole work rests upon faith in God. We make no charge for board or tuition except to let everyone understand that those who have the means are expected to contribute to the support of the word, as the Lord leads. We never ask anybody for anything, and have no church, or society, or individuals to whom to look for support, but depend on God alone.[73]

One must understand the economic conditions of Greenville and surrounding counties in the late 1890s. Greenville was becoming an important center for the cotton mill industry and supplier of mill machinery and parts. Also, the local economies were extremely dependent on agricultural production. The pattern of trust begun in 1898 continues until this day; Jehovah Jireh or our God provides.

After the first term closed, Holmes, S. C. Todd, and M. H. Houston worked the evangelistic trail beginning in Laurens County, S. C. They purchased a large tent for these meetings. Two notable converts during these meetings were L. R. Graham and S. A. Bishop.[74] Holmes recorded that during these meetings, Todd, Houston, and himself began to preach the full gospel of Christ our Savior, Sanctifier, Healer, and coming Lord and King.[75] These meetings continued until December. Holmes recorded a testimony of a convert in Clinton as an example of revival power.

> One man wrote, "I shall have to leave this tent, and stop coming or go to the altar." He went to the altar and got blessed in his soul. God certainly worked wonders in that town in the way of convicting sinners and converting them, sanctifying believers, and healing the sick. Old feuds were settled, old debts were paid, drunkards saved, and delivered from even the appetite for drink....[76]

The Four Fold Gospel was the theological foundation of the Christian and Missionary Alliance. Mattie Perry wrote about a Convention in Goldsboro, N.C., in the June 6, 1897 edition of *The Christian and Missionary Alliance* newspaper.[77] *The Christian and Missionary Alliance* newspaper lists Mattie Perry of Lenior and Rev. John Pike of the Olive Gospel Mission as contacts for Southern Conventions.[78]

Both 1898 and 1899 were important years for Holmes in the formation of his theological foundation, and his involvement thrived central to this development. In June 1898, the CMA held their initial meetings in Greenville, S. C., and then in Laurens. S. C. Todd's home was Laurens, and he was the S. C. State Superintendent for the CMA. J. M. Pike, editor of *The Way of Faith*, hosted the CMA's State Convention. Todd wrote, "At the first service Rev. N. J. Holmes of the Altamont Bible Institute, gave a much blessed address on II Corinthians 3:18."[79] After this meeting, the CMA moved to Greenville, S. C. and held meetings. Brother D. W. Le Lacheur gave his Tibetan talk at First Baptist Church (Greenville). In the audience were the faculty and students of the Altamont Bible Institute, which is located on the summit of Paris Mountain, eight miles away.[80] An important observation for the CMA establishing stations in South Carolina is its influence upon Pike, Holmes, Todd, and Houston. The CMA affiliation of these former ministers to the Presbyterian Church and theology served as a home for them as they discovered other former Presbyterian ministers entering into preaching Holiness and Sanctification in their revival meetings.

The CMA held a Southern Convention in Atlanta, Georgia, from August 18-27, 1899, at the Atlanta Exposition. Several speakers for this Convention besides A. B. Simpson were J. O. McClurkan of Tennessee, Rev. J. M. Pike, M. H. Houston, and N. J. Holmes of South Carolina.[81] Each of these men spread the Four Fold Gospel message as published by Pike's *The Way of Faith*, Holmes, and Houston with the Altamont Bible Institute or McClurkan's Pentecostal Mission in Nashville. The CMA did not yet serve as a denomination but was a uniting influence in the spread of Holiness. In these Conventions, a major message was the recruitment of men and women for missionary work around the world. The Editorial Page of *The Christian and Missionary Alliance* recorded:

> One of the most encouraging features of our work in the South is the attitude of a number of able and influential ministers who are leaders of the Holiness movement and who are encouraging their followers to contribute their missionary funds to the Christian and Missionary Alliance.[82]

Holmes was recorded as holding conventions in Durham and Salem, N. C. and Bennettsville, S. C. Holmes also took charge of the Olive Gospel Mission in Columbia, S. C. The Mission served as a connection with his evangelistic and Altamont Bible Institute.[83]

The second term for the Altamont Bible Institute was changed from a Winter term to a Spring term beginning April 1, 1900, through October 1, 1900, with seven students. The warmer weather provided fewer issues. Anderson wrote, "In the summer—June 25 to July 5 the Institute held a convention."[84] A notable fact was God manifesting His love and power in healing the bodies of the sick.[85] During the second term, Holmes and the staff discussed moving the school to Atlanta. Holmes wrote, "The only work to be done around the mountain was at the county Alms house and a little house on the opposite side of the mountain from the alms house."[86] S. C. Todd recorded the school's move in *The Christian and Missionary Alliance*:

> The purpose of its work is to prepare Christian Workers of all denominations, both male and female, for all kinds of Christian work—in the home and foreign field—to work in the Sunday School, Prayer

Meeting, Revival Service, either as evangelists or helpers. We believe there is a great need in our land for Bible Study and Bible work… can in the shortest time get the most direct training face to face with the Word of God, and under teachers filled with the Holy Ghost."[87]

From December 1899 to January 1900, the Atlanta move was completed to 34 Moreland Avenue. The name was changed to Bible and Missionary Alliance Institute.[88]

The school operated in Atlanta until October 1903; then, the school moved to Columbia, S. C from 1903 to 1905.[89] The school resided in the Olive Branch Mission. Holmes wrote:

> From 1904-1905, a spirit of prayer came upon us for a world revival, and for a month or so, we suspended the daily studies under the burden of protracted prayer. we prayed for a revival, for the manifestation of the Holy Ghost in Pentecostal power for the gifts of the Spirit as promised in 1 Cor. 12: and the signs following in Mark 16.[90]

An important fact for consideration, it appears Holmes, Todd, and Pike broke their affiliation with the CMA sometime in 1900. M. H. Houston continued his CMA work by teaching at Nyack; he eventually retired to Waynesboro, Virginia. Rev. N. J. Holmes and Lucy, Revs. J. M. Pike and S. C. Todd united with Rev. J. O. McClurkan's Pentecostal Mission in Nashville, Tennessee. Holmes was ordained as a Minister, and Lucy was licensed as an Evangelist. Pike was licensed as an Evangelist, and Todd was ordained a Minister. These ministerial commitments took place in 1901 in Atlanta.[91]

The Institute returned to Paris Mountain in October 1905. Holmes wrote:

> We had tried to sell the Altamont property on the mountain, while we were away, but failed, and then we felt that it was the Lord's will for us to return to it. The purpose of the Institute is to train Christian workers of any denomination, whose lives are consecrated to God for Christian work in the home or foreign field.[92]

The South remained in an economic recovery during the Post-Civil War period, so finances to operate a school remained slight to none by student support. A change was made to:

Do away with all stipulated board, and launch out on naked faith in God…We did not believe it would be pleasing to God for those who had no means to hold it back…We determined in the execution of this plan of trusting the whole work to God alone for its support, that we would look to Him alone for its support….[93]

Back to Altamont and Paris Mountain: The Pentecostal Empowerment

The Bible and Missionary Alliance Institute's return to Paris Mountain in 1905 was important for Holmes had sharpened his Holiness preaching and the school's focus. The Christian and Missionary Alliance and the Pentecostal Mission fellowship provided opportunities to build relationships with other Holiness preachers and insights into shaping the Bible school.

After his departure from the South Carolina Presbytery, N. J. and Lucy began an intense study of the Holiness passages from healing in the Atonement and sin's debilitating effects on a person's life. Holmes previously stated all his theology and catechism studies never provided the experience of Scriptural power found in Sanctification and holy living. Until the 1905 return to Altamont each year, his new experiences created a greater desire to understand and obtain the fullness of God.

Upon the school's return to Altamont in 1905, Holmes reflected upon the prayers in Columbia for a worldwide revival. He wrote, "We prayed for a revival of the Holy Ghost in Pentecostal power for the gifts of the Spirit promised in 1 Cor. 12; and the signs following as in Mark 16."[94] Little did he know that the school was drawn into a worldwide symphony of prayer for this Pentecostal outpouring. In India, Pandita Ramabal issued a call for prayer to the women of her ministry at Mukti. Five hundred fifty women met twice daily for intercessory prayer. On June 29, 1905, the women experienced evidence of the Holy Spirit, with several women "slain in the Spirit" and a burning sensation as evidence of their baptism of the Holy Ghost and fire.[95] In 1904-1905 the Welsh Revival was led by Evan Roberts. The Welsh Revival was known for Prayer meetings and services with ecstatic responses to spiritual phenomena.[96] At Nyack, New York, the Christian and Missionary Alliance School teachers and students sensed the leading of the Holy Spirit to enter a season of prayer. This revival of Pentecostal experiences eventually flowed into the town and nearby communities.[97]

Holmes wrote:

> We believed that we had received the baptism with the Holy Ghost
> in sanctification and that it was all one, and what we were praying
> for was not Pentecost or the baptism with the Spirit, but the gifts
> of the Spirit and signs following. God blessed us in our prayers and
> answered them, as far as we met the conditions of the promises at
> that time.[98]

It is important to realize that these early stirrings of the Holy Spirit created
a restorationist impulse. Restorationism is the desire to return to the earliest
days of any movement or the pristine time. Church life and ministry flowed
with the Spirit's gifts bestowed upon all believers. Preaching, teaching, and
evangelism received power from above to accomplish God's desires and purposes.

The Holiness revivals from the 1850s through the early 1900s led various
ministries to publish newsletters and papers. These carried reports of various Spirit visitations to camp meetings, evangelistic meetings on church
grounds, and testimonies of Holiness evangelists. Holmes wrote;

> In the fall of 1906, we saw from some of our religious papers, espe-
> cially, "The Way of Faith," edited by Reverend J. M. Pike, Colum-
> bia, South Carolina, that some of the Lord's people at Los Angeles,
> California and other places, had been praying to God as we had;
> only they seemed to be more definite in their petition, for Pentecost
> with the manifestation of Pentecost—for the baptism with the Holy
> Ghost with the manifestation of speaking in tongues, as it was on
> the day of Pentecost. (Acts 2:4)[99]

These reports from Los Angeles created a greater desire for God. Holmes
reported:

> My heart became more hungry for the manifestation of His pow-
> er, and we began to pray more earnestly for the signs, though we
> still thought we had received the Holy Ghost, yet without the sign
> of tongues.[100] In the midst of spiritual hunger, one of the young
> women of the class, began to praise God with all her heart and soul,
> in a minute was up on her feet praising God, and suddenly began
> talking in an unknown tongue. We were all in quiver in a moment,
> hardly knowing what it was, or what to do.[101]

The question was "this was that." (Acts 2:16) I (Holmes) was glad and rejoiced that something marvelous happened too, and our uncertainty and fear caused us to halt for a season.[102]

Reverend G. B. Cashwell became known as the 'Apostle of Pentecost' in the southeastern United States. Cashwell was a member of The Pentecostal Holiness Church and served in eastern North Carolina. After reading of this new phenomenon in Los Angeles, Cashwell took a train to visit Azusa Street, the location of this ministry. During his visit, he received the Baptism of the Holy Spirit with evidence of speaking in tongues. The Azusa Street people helped purchase his return ticket home in Dunn, NC. He began the meetings in a tobacco warehouse on December 31, 1906. Dunn became known as Azusa Street East. Folks arrived by train and could unload and enter the warehouse. Many pastors responded positively to Cashwell's message on the Baptism of the Holy Spirit. From Dunn Cashwell fanned out across the South with this new message. Several important church leaders, G. F. Taylor and J. H. King of The Pentecostal Holiness Church and A. J. Tomlinson of the Church of God Cleveland, Tennessee, received the Baptism under his ministry.[103]

Holmes went to West Union, South Carolina, for a Cashwell meeting. He recalled:

Others were there who received the Pentecostal baptism and were talking in tongues. Miss Pinky Blake, who had received, led the service. The power of the Holy Ghost came upon her, and she talked in tongues, and sang in tongues some of the sweetest and mostly heavenly music. I was amazed what I saw and heard. I saw she had something that we did not have.[104]

The confusion for Holmes resided in the Holiness teachings that sanctification included the Baptism. This teaching was common among the advocates of Holiness preaching and ministry. Once again, Holmes recalled:

I thought and testified that I had received the baptism with the Holy Ghost, and I could not seek what I believed I already had, so I did not go. (altar call)...I thought I should receive the signs and manifestation now, as I had already received the baptism, and the evidence of it, so I got nothing from the meeting.[105]

Holmes returned to Altamont and explained the meeting to the students. He taught his position concerning the Holy Spirit and sanctification's work. Miss Lida Purkey, one of the teachers, attended the West Union meeting and returned speaking in tongues.

An invitation for Miss Pinkie Blake was extended to minister at Altamont. Confusion continued as the students searched the Scriptures and Greek lexicons for more understanding. It seemed fear, confusion, and thirst for the deeper ways of God consumed the teachers and students. After the third day, Sister Blake said to me, "Well Brother Holmes we feel that the Lord would have us go. We have done all we know to do, and I feel the Holy Spirit is grieved. The responsibility of this Institute, and this truth of Pentecost is upon you."[106] Looking back now, this word from Miss Blake issued a positive exhortation for Holmes.

Holmes recalled, "For my part I was getting disturbed about my theology."[107] So Holmes entered a prolonged fast with Bible study and prayer over the Baptism. During this fast, he wrote, "Now Lord, I do not know, I ask thee to show me the truth, I will put my theology up on the shelf, and let it stay there until you show me what to take down. Give me the truth as it is in Christ."[108] This first step in surrender was greeted by a sister addressing Holmes with an exhortation of "Get the Holy Ghost, get the Holy Ghost," three times.[109] Holmes was experiencing a similar situation as J. H. King faced at Toccoa Falls, Georgia, over the Baptism. King sought all passages of Scripture and used his Greek Lexicon to understand this new manifestation.[110] Holmes laboring over Scriptural understating finally brought a breakthrough. Once again, he penned:

> I soon reached the point where I could see that sanctification was not Pentecost, and that what I received was the Holy Spirit in sanctifying grace and power, but not the Pentecostal endowment…Pentecost is the receiving the promise of the Father, the endowment with power from on high…Sanctification is love, character. The baptism with the Holy Ghost is power, service.[111]

Monday, April 22, 1907, found Holmes in a prayer service at school. He felt a burden to seek his Heavenly Father for the fullness of the Spirit. L. R. Graham led the prayer service as Holmes yielded his spirit to the Holy Spirit. His Baptism event descended from heaven:

I felt my tongue slightly moving up and down, the motion grew stronger and stronger. I was conscious that it was not I, that did it, and I was sure that it was the Holy Ghost, and immediately my teeth began to chatter without my effort or control, and continued for some time…The Holy Ghost came to abide with me.[112]

Miss Pinkie Blake's exhortation for the Institute was upon Holmes' shoulders concerning the acceptance of the Baptism with tongues as Holmes' experience flowed upon other students. Oscar Taylor, a student, and L. R. Graham, a teacher, soon received the blessing. Yet the entire Institute remained in question over the Baptism.

On June 1, 1907, the Institute began Commencement exercises with a week-long commitment to prayer and devotional exercises. Reverend G. F. Taylor, principal of the Falcon School in North Carolina, was the chosen minister for the Commencement. During the week, no special manifestations came upon the attendees. Taylor's final message for the Institute came from John 7:37-39, "If any man thirst, let him come unto me and drink." The hearts of the students were stirred, and conviction of the Spirit descended upon the students. Taylor closed the service with a call for the baptism with the Holy Ghost. In his altar call, Taylor speaking of the Holy Ghost said, "You may afford to do without it; I could not."[113] Immediately, the Holy Ghost fell upon the hearers, and soon students began to speak in tongues. Holmes recounted the manifestations:

Some of them here and there in the tent began to rise up speaking in tongues. Some began to write in unknown languages, some were singing in other tongues, others dancing, and others playing on the organ under the power of the Spirit. Pentecost had indeed come to Altamont. During the day there were fifteen, who received the baptism and spoke in other tongues….[114]

Lucy Holmes received the Baptism the next day. Some students remained questioning this new experience versus their teaching on sanctification.

Once again, the Holmes took to the evangelistic trail after the school's closing. These ministry appointments met with either openness or rejection concerning tongues-speaking as evidence of the Holy Spirit Baptism. Holmes joined with Cashwell in Clinton, South Carolina, for a meeting. God moved mightily as many were saved, sanctified, and some received their Pentecost. S. A. Bishop, a student at Altamont, received his Pentecostal experience.[115] The evangelistic tour took them to the Falcon Camp Meeting and to various churches in Laurens County. Laurens has been called the Home of Pentecost for South Carolina.

The new school year for the Bible School arrived for the Fall semester. The Holmes returned from their summer evangelistic tour in the South. One important feature of these summer tours was recruiting students and raising attention for donations to fund the school. N. J. Holmes was known for his sincere devotion to Jesus as well as a powerful proclaimer of God's Word. The school decided to postpone its opening until the Rev. and Mrs. Holmes returned from the Nashville Convention of the Pentecostal Mission.

As the Pentecostal Baptism teaching crossed the country, several Pentecostal Mission folks accepted this new teaching. At the 1907 Annual Convention of the Pentecostal Mission in Nashville, the "Tongues Controversy" became a focus for the Mission's doctrinal position. On the October 5th afternoon session, Holmes delivered a powerful sermon. The Minutes of 1907 recorded, "(At the close) N. J. Holmes, president of the Altamont Bible School in South Carolina, made a fervent appeal for missionaries."[116] Sunday, October 6, Holmes preached the night service; it is recorded, "A number were at the altar seeking pardon and purity."[117]

During the Annual Convention, McClurkan confronted the 'Tongues Issue" and maintained the position of Sanctification was the Baptism of the Holy Spirit. W. T. Purkiser, a Nazarene theologian, summed up the Pentecostal Mission's position on tongues:

There is virtually no basis for equating Pentecost with the phenomenon of glossolalia, either in its modern expression or as some have thought to implied by the reference to a gift of languages in 1 Corinthians 12 and problematic in 1 Corinthians 14.[118]

Purkiser continued his Biblical and historical overview, "It is fair to say that in the historical or dispensational sense, Pentecost has not and can not be repeated. Any historical era can have only one beginning."[119] As the proponents of Tongues left the Pentecostal Mission, O. N. Todd, Jr. wrote, "that as painful as the separation was, they all parted in love and kindness."[120]

The empowerment of the Holy Spirit descended at the Bible School's Spring

Commencement services and brought a fresh spirit of experiencing the manifestation of the Spirit almost continually on Altamont. Holmes recalled, "Thus the term began, and from beginning to end, it was a continuous lesson of God's grace, love, providence, and supernatural manifestation of His divine power. It was, to me, and I believe to many others, the most blessed and soul-inspiring season I had ever passed through. There was hardly a day from beginning to the close, eight months, but there was some visible or perceptible manifestation of the blessed Holy Ghost."[121]

In the early days of the Pentecostal outpouring, pastors, teachers, missionaries, and lay people attended a daily school in devotional life for interpreting and moving with the Spirit's gift operations. Zeal for God reached new heights, but with zeal follows proper discipline. Henry Rack's book on John Wesley, *Reasonable Enthusiast,* provided careful insights into Wesley's ministry in teaching and preaching among people of healthy and proper Spirit operations. The school began the term with roughly fifty students and teachers, "nearly all of them had received their Pentecost before they came or received it after they came.[122]

Tongues operation and interpretation required a discerning ear and spirit. Many spoken words dealt with the second coming of Jesus Christ, and some directed attention to rebuking evil spirits from disrupting the school and its ministry. The Baptism of the Holy Spirit with tongues opened a new door into the battle of the powers and principalities in the heavens that required the students to maintain a teachable spirit. Holmes wrote, "Nothing that has come in my life has enabled me to realize the presence and power of God as Pentecost has."[123]

The school term closed on June 1, 1908, with Commencement exercises and preaching. Again Holmes recorded, "During which time several received the baptism with the Holy Ghost, including a missionary from Corea (sic)."[124]

N. J. and Lucy continued their summer pattern of evangelistic meetings across the South at school's end. The evangelistic summer tours focused on Atlanta, Georgia, the mountains of North Carolina in Culbertson and Asheville, and Birmingham, Alabama. A team of students and a teacher traveled with the Holmes to various areas. The first meeting was in Atlanta at the Pentecostal Mission. Mrs. E. A. Sexton provided hospitality for the Holmes and company. She was the editor of *The Bridegroom's Messenger.*[125]

G. B. Cashwell founded this paper that became the information center for Pentecostal articles and meetings in the South. *The Bridegroom's Messenger* and *The Way of Faith* provided insights into the Pentecostal Movement around the nation.

In 1908 *The Way of Faith* Directors attempted to remove the Pentecostal news. The Board pressed heavily on J. M. Pike, the Editor, for a return to publishing only news of the Holiness Movement. *The Daily Record* of Columbia, South Carolina, carried the report of this internal battle. The article addressed:

> The "Healing by Faith" and the "Unknown Tongues" movement, which has strong and influential advocates at several points in the State, particularly Laurens, where members of the oldest and most prominent families in the State are its active and most zealous supporters gained an important victory in a high place here in Columbia this week....[126]

Rev. J. M. Pike vigorously defended the Pentecostal articles. The readership of the paper was roughly 10,000, and 9/10 of those readers would not tolerate removing these articles on Pentecostalism. Pike also said that the readership covered the United States and other parts of the world.[127] The Board yielded to Pike's position. This Board's misunderstanding was repeated among other Holiness publications as, again, understanding the Baptism of the Holy Spirit with evidence of tongues was a separate crisis moment.

After closing the Atlanta meeting, Holmes and Sister Nellie Lane went to Culbertson, North Carolina, for meetings. Holmes' team joined with Miss Mamie Leopard, one of the school's teachers, in these services. Holmes recorded, "That was a hard cold place in the mountains, where there were only two people who believed in sanctification, Sister Anderson and Sister Massey.[128] From Culbertson, the evangelistic team traveled to Hayesville for meetings. Large turnouts for the preaching encouraged the team, but many left, and some became interested in the gifts of the Spirit. On return to Altamont, they traveled to Simpsonville for a series of meetings. The last tour took them to Birmingham, Alabama, for meetings with Brother M. M. Pinson. Holmes remembered:

> This was the most largely attended meeting we had during the summer...Many were blessed, some saved, some sanctified, and some

received the baptism of the Holy Ghost and spoke in other tongues. There were some remarkable manifestations of the Holy Spirit's work.[129]

Before returning to Altamont's school opening, the team attended the meeting of the Southern Pentecostal Association. Holmes was named President. The object of the Association was to promote the truths of the deeper Christian life, including sanctification, divine healing, and Pentecost, and also to promote the cause of missions in the foreign field, as well as the homeland.[130]

Each new school year opened the doors for understanding God's gifts and manifestations among students' preparations for ministry as a pastor, teacher, missionary, or layperson. The Bible and Missionary Institute opened on October 1, 1908, with nearly seventy students at one point. Holmes wrote, "There was in some ways a deeper work of the Holy Ghost; at least it was brought out more through interpretation and discernment."[131] A larger student body meant greater trust in God to provide monies for food, supplies, and the maintenance of the property. During worship or prayer services, greater attention was given to testings and trials. Holmes observed:

> Sometimes the enemy got in some of his work in imitation of the work of the Spirit, and it took discernment of the Holy Spirit to distinguish between the imitation and the real. Thank God, He knows, and can teach us the difference if we are obedient and attentive to Him.[132]

The Commencement Services in May 1909 laid new ground for the school's future.

Holmes and several students went to Greenville and studied a plot of land for the purpose of building a small tabernacle. N. J. and Lucy owned a lot roughly an acre in size in the northwestern part of the city. Looking toward the future, N. J. wrote, "Where we might if the Lord willed, build a tabernacle for service, and eventually have a school or college where those who desired, might be taught other branches of learning."[133] Holmes' mother's vision appeared as expanding the ability to educate larger groups of students for Christian work. The tabernacle was shaped in the form of a cross, and measurements were thirty by sixty feet each way. Holmes traded a small lot to the West End Lumber Company for $400.00 of lumber, then another

$100.00 near the end of construction. He awakened one morning with the original plan for the tabernacle and thought, "Better to build now than to add on in the future." Students and friends of the city joined in constructing the building. The women students, along with Lucy, cooked meals and aided work in other areas.[134] Suddenly, this expansion opened an opportunity for ministry among the mill folks around the tabernacle and prepared the way for a new school location.

Erection of the tabernacle progressed smoothly, and the Holmes took to the evangelistic trail from Birmingham to Franklin, Tennessee, and Dixon Springs, Tennessee. Miss Mary Smithson and Miss Nina Cotton aided the Holmes in the ministry meetings at these locations. Messages in tongues and singing followed the team from place to place. Other workers with the Holmes were Misses Anna Dean Cole, Annie Lamar, Janie Milton, and Ellen Trepard.[135] These helpers, like farmers, sowed seed for the harvest, but the harvest was the Gospel seed of Full Salvation.

In the years 1909 through 1910, attendance grew, and a greater emphasis developed in the understanding of the Spirit's work. One of the highlights was Miss Fay Watson, a teacher, receiving the call for the mission field. Rev. and Mrs. Richard Anderson returned from the mission field of Central America for rest and health. The Andersons visited Altamont, and two blessings happened. First, the Andersons received the Baptism of the Holy Spirit with tongues, and second, Brother Anderson was healed of appendicitis. Rev. Holmes began preaching in the tabernacle every Sunday. He would take several students as helpers in the ministry. Richard Sawgalsky, a Russian Jew, was the first person saved in the tabernacle.[136] A decision was made to change the school calendar of operation from winter to summer, with the new opening in May 1910 through December.[137]

As the school year for 1910 began, Holmes was sixty-two years old. He continued teaching the Bible with a love for the types and shadows of the Jewish sacrifices and the tabernacle structure. G. F. Taylor recalled in 1910, Rev. Holmes organized the Tabernacle Church in Greenville. Later several organizations followed under the same name as Tabernacle. Later, these churches formed the Southern Pentecostal Association, whose purpose was to support pastors, send missionaries, and conduct evangelistic meetings.[138] Lucy Holmes recalled:

Mr. Holmes has said he was sure no one had ever gone up and down that mountain as often as he and I had. In the little buggy with the faithful gray horse—in the hottest summer sunshine or the coldest winter wind, or snow, sometimes so deep the buggy step would plough through the drifts…we have gone up and down the mountain in the service of God and found pleasure in it.[139]

As the couple aged, they spent their winters in a room in the Tabernacle.

On March 22, 1911, Rev. Holmes conducted a double wedding in the Tabernacle for Mr. Paul F. Beacham and Miss Sarah Nell Lane and Mr. Zelotes L. Holmes to Miss Nina Lillian Cotton. Zelotes was Holmes' nephew, and Rev. Holmes hoped his nephew would become the next leader of the Bible school. Mr. Beacham continued his work in the school and eventually became the Old and New Testament teacher. On October 23, 1911, the Altamont Bible and Missionary Training Institute began publishing *The Altamont Witness*. Each publication contained teachings by the Institute teachers and letters from the saints and missionaries. Lucy Holmes wrote:

We hope to bear witness, with others of "like precious faith," as He may enable us, to the great, fundamental truths of the Word of God—Regeneration, Sanctification, Divine Healing, and the Pentecostal Baptism with the Holy Ghost.[140]

In October 1912, Rev. Holmes contracted a severe cold and cough as he aided in taking down a tent.[141] This sickness began a gradual failing of his health. He continued his regular duties of running the Institute, preaching, and his travels for evangelistic meetings.

Holmes Final Years 1914-1919

As the summer of 1914 began, Holmes was again traveling to various locations to hold revival meetings. This discipline of summer preaching fulfilled his earnest desire to fulfill the role of an evangelist since his resignation from the Second Presbyterian Church in Spartanburg. In July 1914, he joined A.A. Boddy, J. H. King, and S. A. Bishop for a camp meeting in Atlanta. Upon his return to Greenville, he suffered a fall from the porch of the Tabernacle. As he sat in a chair to read the newspaper, he leaned against a rail that was not nailed properly to the porch. Now seventy years old, he suffered severe bruising. Holmes was scheduled to preach at a camp meeting in Chocowinity of eastern North Carolina. Fully bruised and suffering, Lucy wasn't feeling well enough to travel with him, so Brother T. A. Melton, one of the students, traveled with him.[142]

The year 1915 became an important year for Holmes as he not only continued this camp meeting schedule but an important decision was reached for moving the campus to Briggs Avenue. Holmes' first summer excursion took them to Falcon, N. C. to preach the closing exercises of the Falcon Holiness School. These services united G. F. Taylor and his wife, Ella, with the Holmes again. Holmes held the graduation services at the Bethel Holiness School in Rose Hill, N. C. in the spring of 1905.[143]

Toward the closing school term in 1914, the school's future became a consideration of remaining on Paris Mountain or moving. Mrs. Lucy Holmes recorded these considerations:

> Toward the close of that term of school a strong desire seemed to take possession of the school, first the teachers, and then the students, that the school must leave the mountain and be transferred to the city of Greenville.[144]

A vote was taken by the teachers and students, with all positive for the move and two against changing locations. This new adventure meant sacrifice for the Altamont family as workers, cooks, and others aiding in the new construction.

Lucy wrote:

> Mr. Holmes said if the boys would agree to stay and give a month's work on the building, he would try to furnish the lumber. This was done, God in some way providing the funds. Most of the boys agreed to stay and the girls went home except a few who stayed and helped in the necessary cooking, etc., and we came to Greenville.[145]

Rev. Holmes secured Brother John T. Dempsey as the foreman and Fred Witherspoon as the brick mason. God gave His witness for this new project by providing funds and supplies to construct the building for bedrooms and the boy's study hall. Holmes had a vision for a girls' dormitory plus a dining hall with a kitchen. The first building was completed in two months. As the

Institute moved to Greenville, the school was renamed the Holmes Bible and Missionary Institute.[146] With the dormitory completed, school began on February 1, 1916.[147]

The horror of World War I pressed upon everyone from lack of building supplies, labor, and concern for our nation. Rev. Holmes suffered from strange pressure in his head, severe coughing since 1912, and fainting episodes. The Pentecostal Holiness Church approached Rev. Holmes about a merger of the Tabernacle churches in 1915. Several churches merged with the Pentecostal Holiness Church, such as Gum Springs, SC, Long Branch, SC, Birmingham, AL., and Easley, SC, but Holmes maintained the Tabernacle separately.[148] The Institute's missionaries became Pentecostal Holiness missionaries in the merger.[149] In May 1916, Holmes struggled to maintain a camp meeting schedule. He made a few trips. He attended camp meeting as a delegated speaker along with J. H. King and Mr. Sawgalsky. Miss Nina Holmes accompanied Rev. and Mrs. Holmes in their meetings. Upon return in October, Rev. Holmes became a father to the students. As Lucy wrote:

> He often made good talks to the students encouraging, counseling, and trying to impress upon them the importance of a well-rounded Christian character. He maintained attendance for the Friday night prayer meetings as on the mountain and preaching once on Sundays.[150]

Rev. Holmes was a steady witness of God's grace and mercy not only for the students but his influence upon the southern Pentecostal movement.

World War I ended in 1917 with the Allies defeating the Germans. The war's toil upon all nations produced sorrow for the thousands of young lives lost, the destruction of various European lands, and a punishing Treaty of Versailles upon the Germans and restructure of the European map. Rev. Holmes daily read the newspapers with interest in the war's development and end. The 1917 Commencement Services and camp meeting found Revs. S. A. Bishop, G. F. Taylor, and J. H. King as the guest speakers. Exhausted by the closing services, Rev. and Mrs. Holmes, Mrs. Nina Holmes, and Brother Morgan retreated to Paris Mountain for recuperation. The Altamont retreat provided recovery for the Holmes to attend a camp meeting in Birmingham, Alabama. Rev. S. A. Bishop and his wife provided wonderful hospitality for the Holmes. Rev. Holmes, though feeble and weak of speech, delivered several messages. The aging Gospel warrior drew his strength from God to exhort hearers for salvation, sanctification, and the Baptism of the Holy Spirit.

The new school year beginning on October 1, 1918, found the Bible and Missionary Institute for its twentieth year. The enrollment listed forty students. Lucy remembered:

> Numbers of the soldiers were about everywhere, from Camp Sevier, and some attended our Tabernacle services and some visited us. Mr. Holmes preached occasionally though not really able to preach with his old time energy, and had different students to preach at different times.[151]

At school's ending, the Holmes retreated to Paris Mountain for rest. The couple returned home on Briggs Avenue in July, and Miss Katherine Holmes, a trained nurse, came and provided care for Rev. Holmes. His health declined, as his schedule became selective for his presence requested for events. He spent his days in quiet repose and reading. Just after the new school 1918-1919 year began, Rev. Holmes suffered a complete health breakdown.

The summer ritual of returning to Paris Mountain for rest appeared the Holmes' last trip to their cottage. In 1918 they sold the building and property for $5000.00. With the attachment to Paris Mountain and Altamont, the family retired to Briggs Avenue. Miss Julia Payne, a missionary to China and former student, cared for the Holmes. The Franklin Springs camp meeting approached in August, and he wished to attend. Lucy wrote:

> Finally we decided to go, if Miss Julia would go with us. And we left home on Wednesday to be gone until Monday. We found many old students of the Holmes Bible and Missionary Institute there—forty, I believe attended the meeting—and many volunteers for foreign missions present, and all but one were Institute students.[152]

G. F. and Ella Taylor provided the hospitality during this visit. After Monday's breakfast, Rev. Holmes left breakfast, and as he leaned over the porch railing, he fell and dislocated his right hip. Two weeks later, they returned home by car.

Two months later, on October 21, 1919, he suffered another nervous collapse and never recovered. Taylor wrote in the Memorial Issue of Holmes,

"For several days I heard an inward voice that could not be hushed, saying, 'Go see Brother Holmes next Friday, it is your last chance.'"[153] Taylor and his wife, Ella, left Franklin Springs on December 5 for the final visit. He remembered Rev. Holmes' final words to him, then painted this final scene, "What a heavenly countenance, what tender words that fell from his lips, how comforting the glance of his eye." Reverend Nickels John Holmes entered his final rest on December 19, 1919. His mother's vision of a Bible training school, his sister Olive's words "Preach the Gospel," and his influence upon numerous folks with his teaching and preaching now rested in fulfillment of God's Will.

Holmes Bible College Images

Historic Campuses

The Oliver Mission Bldg in
Columbia SC Jan 1903-Jun 1905

Staff and Students of Holmes at
Oliver Mission in Columbia. SC

Altamont Missionary and
Bible Institute 1909

Tabernacle on Briggs behind
where Holmes Memorial
was built

Lucy Holmes Admin
Bldg 115 Briggs Ave

Holmes Memorial
Tabernacle Pentecostal
Church

Trailerville on Briggs Ave 1956

The WD Reynolds
Boys Dorm on Old
Buncombe Street

The Girls Dorm, Chapel, and
Dining Hall

New Campus

Entrance - Shaw-Leslie Campus

Holmes Memorial Tabernacle
Pentecostal Church

Paul Franklin Beacham
Learning Center

Tripp-Van Dyke Residence
Hall for Men

Freeman-Duncan
Dormitory for Women

The Brooks-King Mission
Duplex

The Ellenberg Student Center

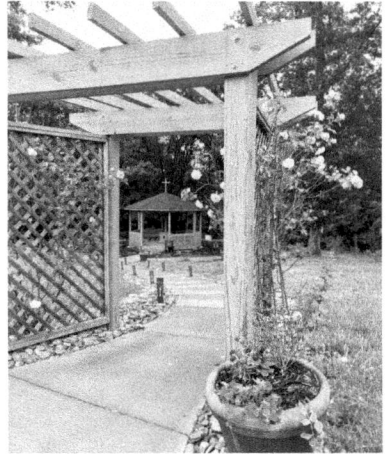

Richard D. and Ella L. Waters
Prayer and Missions Garden

Carl O. Sturkie
Maintenance Building

President's Home

3. Continuing The Vision of Reverend N. J. Holmes:1920 to the Present

Paul F. Beacham, President 1920-1978

Paul F. Beacham was born on September 18, 1888, near Westminster, South Carolina, to Mr. and Mrs. Archibald L. Beacham. During his youth, he worked in a mill near Honea Path. His oldest brother, Hartwell Beacham, was a brotherly witness to accept Jesus Christ as his Savior. He attended local schools but felt the need to receive more education. Hartwell encouraged Paul to attend Holmes Bible and Missionary. Paul began his student life at Altamont in 1908. Immediately he became known for his trustworthiness as a student and helper. As Rev. Holmes' health declined, Paul became the Old and New Testament teacher. Eventually, Holmes elevated him to Business Manager for the school, and in 1911, he became the Editor of *The Altamont Witness*. Rev. Holmes named Brother Beacham to be his successor. Upon Rev. Holmes' death on December 19, 1919, Paul F. Beacham assumed the Presidency.[154]

Under President Beacham's leadership, the school grew to great heights numerically and in campus buildings. His first endeavor was the 1921 construction of a girls' dormitory that was a fulfillment of Holmes' vision. The Holmes Memorial Church was erected in 1924 and opened for services in 1925. Beacham served as the Pastor from 1919 until 1978.

The Holmes residence became home for school offices after the death of Mrs. Lucy Holmes. In 1937, the home's renovation provided an office for the President, classrooms, and the library. The home was given the name of

"The White House." In 1938 a decision was made to enlarge and remodel the girls' dormitory. Mr. Alvin Rankin came to the school in 1938. He held a B.S. in Mechanical Engineering. Mr. Rankin's talents were greatly appreciated and used in remodeling and erecting new structures on campus. He was acknowledged for his thirty-two years of service to the school. He recalled living by faith as his and Mrs. Rankin's salary was $9.00 a year. In 1969 the Rankins resided at 109 Briggs Avenue in a home. They recalled living in one place and moving seven times over the years. They spoke of their new home, "It is the first time they have had a back porch and yard. We thank the Lord for it."[155]

Rev. Paul F. and Sara L. Beacham

The summer of 1941 found a new men's dormitory needful as men's applications increased for the school. With the help of students and friends, this construction was completed in 1942. As each new building or remodeling project commenced, President Beacham upheld Rev. Holmes' commitment to being debt free.[156] Rev. S. Lee Braxton appealed to the former students and friends to join in providing building funds for the new Boys' Dormitory. He wrote:

Every year there are scores of applicants turned away because a dormitory room is not available. Someone made it possible for you to attend this school—now let us make it possible for others. $6,000.00 is needed at once to complete the rooms and install the plumbing and heating plant.[157]

Mr. Braxton continued, "I would put a conservative value of over $30,000.00 on this building when completed—just think, only $6,000.00 needed to finish the building for the next term!'[158] A miracle in this construction was the availability of construction materials as needed due to supply shortages during World War II. One means of obtaining funds was using Coin Albums. Each album contained $5.00 in nickels, dimes, and quarters.[159]

On October 8, 1942, the Holmes Bible School opened for its 44th term. President Beacham welcomed everyone for the new school year and used Luke 9:51-52 as the guiding Scripture for the year. Another new announcement was establishing a B. A. Degree in Bible Education. Mrs. Nell Beacham, Editor of *The Holmes College Bulletin*, sought 2,000 more good books for the library.

As World War II ended, the returning soldiers sought a means to higher education, and the G. I. Bill passed by Congress provided funds to accomplish this goal. Holmes received approval for acceptance from the G. I. Bill. In 1947, the school purchased ten lots on Briggs Avenue, providing room for roughly twenty-five homes. Married families began to apply for study at Holmes, thus increasing housing needs for these people.[160] Rev. F. V. Ellenberg assumed the task of purchasing needed equipment for the school and 18 trailers. The new housing on campus became Trailerville. The new veteran students provided the grading and digging ditches for water pipes and sewage lines.[161] Brother J. L. Pruitt served as the superintendent.[162] Rev. Ellenberg estimated the value of this equipment near $50,000. Holmes became a Church Seminary in an announcement in April 1947. The announcement became official as *The Voice of Holmes* published:

> Holmes Bible College became the recognized and approved seminary of the Pentecostal Holiness Church on March 3, 1947, on the merits of its record of 50 years of work in preparing men and women for real Christian service and more than 30 years the church training most of her ministers and missionaries.

The General Board of Administration approved this move in Toronto, Ontario, Canada.[163]

As 1947 closed, the sad news reached the Holmes students, former students, and friends about the death of Mrs. Sarah Lane Beacham. Mrs. Beacham attended the school at Altamont in 1905 and became a trusted camp meeting helper with the Holmes in their summer travels. She joined the faculty in

1911 and taught Theology and Missions classes. Her work, *Men and Missions*, became the textbook for the missions classes.[164]

The Twenty-third Annual Convention assembled on May 19-20, 1949. This Convention of the Holmes Alumni Association embraced former students from many states, and their speakers were Bishop T. A. Melton and Bishop J. A. Synan. The Association had a large Gospel tent erected on campus for the speakers. During the meeting, Brother R. B. Phillips, a former student and brick mason, was acknowledged for his brickwork on the Lucy Holmes Memorial Building and his laying the cornerstone for its commemoration.

President Paul F. Beacham presided over the growth of Holmes and witnessed, in 1947, a student body of two hundred sixty-one students. In 1958 the Charter was amended, and the name changed to Holmes Theological Seminary.[165]

President Beacham's career included several ministerial accomplishments. He was a charter member of the Tabernacle Presbyterian Church in 1910, along with distinguished ministers such as; Reverends L. R. Graham, S. A. Bishop, and W. A. Anderson. These men experienced the Baptism of the Holy Spirit after Rev. G. F. Taylor's Commencement Services in the spring of 1907. Holmes changed the church name to the Tabernacle Pentecostal Church. Rev. Beacham joined the other ministers of the Tabernacle Pentecostal Church after the Canon, Georgia meeting joined with the Pentecostal Holiness Church in 1915. Beacham became a member of the Upper South Carolina Conference and remained a member for sixty-three years. He was elected at the 1921 General Conference to the General Board of the Pentecostal Holiness Church. In 1925 he was chosen to the General Board as the General Treasurer. As General Treasurer, his service tallied for twenty years for the denomination. His responsibilities required paying all bills, including missionaries' salaries and field expenses. Later, Rev. Beacham directed the Missions Department of the church.[166]

In 1946 Rev. Hubert T. Spence resigned from the Bishop's position, and Rev. Beacham was appointed by the General Board of Administration to fill the vacancy. He served as Bishop for three years. Later positions held by Rev. Beacham were Editor of the *Advocate*, the official church newspaper, and editor of the Adult Sunday School Quarterly. His writing career found him as the author of *Questions and Answers on the Bible and Related Subjects* and *Meat in Due Season*. He remained a popular camp meeting and Bible Conference Speaker throughout his life. His understanding of the Scriptures was the hallmark of his speaking and teaching career. Bishop S. A. Synan wrote in the Memorial issue:

> Paul Franklin Beacham has made a lasting contribution to his denomination and left an enduring impression for good upon it...Let us pray that his Lord and ours, the Lord of the Church, will raise up someone who, with God's blessing, may at least in part fill this gap in our rank.[167]

Rev. Paul F. Beacham crossed the River Jordan to rest from his labors on February 13, 1978.

Dr. Kenneth D. Benson 1978-1996

Kenneth Benson made his way to Holmes in 1952 as he worked his way across the Atlantic on a Swedish freighter, the Parramatta. Brother Benson was born on June 15, 1932, in Pretoria, South Africa, to A. J. Benson and Martha Roos Benson. He received a Th. B from Holmes Bible College and a Bachelor of Arts in Bible from Southern Wesleyan University. He also received an Honorary Doctorate Degree from Holmes Bible College.[168] After his graduation from Holmes, he served as the Associate Pastor at Holmes Memorial Church and taught classes at the School.

In 1957 Brother Benson joined the Western NC Conference of the Pentecostal Holiness

Rev. Kenneth D. and Dorothy A. Benson

Church. He became an evangelist for one year. Dr. Benson received an appointment to First Pentecostal Holiness in Charlotte, North Carolina. He served fourteen years as the pastor until he received a call from Holmes to return and teach Old and New Testament classes. Upon President Beacham's death in 1978, Dr. Benson was appointed President and assumed the role of Lead Pastor of Holmes Memorial.[169]

Dr. Benson's lasting contribution to Holmes Bible College centered on "biblical balance." Students remembered him as "the greatest of Bible teachers." Also, a major accomplishment of his Presidency came in the form of Faculty and Staff receiving remuneration. During Dr. Benson's term, he never accepted a salary from the College.[170] A shocking announcement arrived on campus as the Fall Semester of 1996 began that Dr. Benson's health required his retirement as President. After his retirement, the Board of Trustees honored Dr. Benson with President Emeritus. On March 2, 2011, the College was notified that Dr. Benson went home with the Lord Jesus Christ.

Dr. Richard M. Waters 1996-2008

Rev. Richard M. and Maxine C. Waters

In 1996 the Board of Trustees of Holmes elevated Dr. Richard Waters from Dean of Academics at Holmes to become the fourth President of the Holmes College of the Bible. Dr. Richard Waters came with strong educational credentials with a Major in Electrical Engineering from North Carolina State University, a Bachelor of Arts in Religion from North Carolina Wesleyan College, a Master of Divinity from Duke Divinity School of Duke University, and a Doctorate of Ministry from The Graduate Seminary of Phillips University. He earned Academic Honors from N. C. State University, Honors in Religion at N. C. Wesleyan College, and an Honors Graduate from Duke Divinity School. He is listed in the Who's Who in Religion in America.

His Academic career included serving as the Professor of Old and New Testament, Church History, and Christian Ethics at Southwestern College. Dr. Waters later became Vice President for Academic Affairs at Southwestern College of Christian Ministries.

Dr. Waters is an Ordained Minister in the International Pentecostal Holiness Church. He was Associate Pastor at Grace Chapel PH Church in Oklahoma City and had the distinction of being Associate Pastor of Duke Chapel of Duke University in Durham, N. C. Dr. Waters served on the General Level of the I.P.H.C. as a member of Church Institutions and Chairman of the Education Committee for the Oklahoma Conference I.P.H.C.

He served on the Full Life Study Bible Editorial Committee (Commentary and Special Articles), Lockman Foundation: Editorial Committee for the New Standard Rainbow Study Bible, and N.A.S.B. Topical Reference Bible.

Dr. Waters' wealth of experience from Educational to Ecclesiastical Service enabled him to guide Holmes as the 21st century approached with new ventures in education.

The Ingathering '97 found alumni and friends gathering at the College to celebrate one of the most important days for Holmes Bible College. From singing to preaching, the Ingathering was a great success. For the first time, attendees heard online from two alumni serving as missionaries. Rev. Kit Teasdale serving in South Africa, and Rev. Rodney Bohler, a missionary to the Crow Indians in Hardin, Montana. All celebrated the work of these missionaries and all missionaries serving Jesus Christ around the world. All donations for the College totaled $63,000. Then in November, students joined in Phone-a-thon '97. They received pledges of $11,735 from 495 people. The money went into the Gap Scholarship program to fund the difference between the rising costs of education and the amount students can pay.[171]

Ingathering 2000 received more than 200 alumni and friends. The pledges and gifts totaled $70.000. President Waters expressed thankfulness to all who participated in the Faculty Christmas Fund. The most exciting news announced the Mission, Vision, and Goals. The Short-term Goals (1-3 years) listed:

1. Increase enrollment to 105 annually.

2. Faculty and Staff remuneration to develop a faculty composed pri-

marily of full-time personnel.

3. Expand Christian Education, Communications, and Distance Learning.

4. Advancement to develop a larger pool of sustained donors and will planning with capital funds for relocation.

The Long-term goals (5-10 years) consisted of:

1. A long-term goal of 500 students,

2. Faculty and Staff remuneration for salaries with similar colleges recognized by the Accrediting Association of Bible Colleges,

3. Relocation and new campus,

4. An Endowment program for scholarships, academic chairs, and campus maintenance, and

5. Accreditation.[172]

In May, an announcement revealed 90% of the $1.2 million in gifts and pledges had been paid toward the campus relocation. Also, Chris Thompson and Richard E. Porterfield became members of the Board.[173]

An important outreach program initiated a vision for personal and social transformation in its own neighborhood as the College pursued its relocation. This program continues Rev. Holmes' vision to reach people in every neighborhood with the Gospel. Holmes Bible College offered 2,250-3,000 volunteer hours of service per year. The school worked with the Greenville Rescue Mission, the Salvation Army Boys & Girls, the American Leprosy Mission, United Missions, Place of Hope, and the Christian Blind Mission International. Students received Christian service hours; the experience training them to be effective change agents in the community.[174]

President Waters' leadership saw the initial Off-campus classes. Dr. Parnell Coward taught 1 and 2 Corinthians. Radice Banks taught the Philosophy of Christian Education, and Ann Hitt led studies in Small Group Ministry. Ingathering 2002 welcomed Bishop James D. Leggett, the General Superintendent of the International Pentecostal Holiness Church as the guest speaker. The Ingathering 2002 Giving Report recorded $59,859.11 in gifts and pledges. These offerings provided nearly 20% of the school's unrestricted income for the year. The wonderful announcement was Mr. Jimmy

Thompson, owner of WGGS-TV, Channel 16, in Greenville, offered time to hold a Holmes Telethon to raise funds for campus relocation. President Waters said:

> We'll be reaching an audience through the Telethon that might not have known about Holmes before. The show will be picked up in numerous towns in various parts of the country and will give us a good opportunity to tell our story.

Brother Thompson graduated from Holmes, and in 1956 he completed his B. A. degree at Furman University. He pastored Faith Temple for 30 years until his retirement.[175]

The Board, in October 2004, announced new developments on campus relocation. The new campus name approved by the Board was the Leslie-Shaw campus of Holmes Bible College, as the Leslie and Shaw families provided significant contributions to Holmes. The entrance, water fountain, and gated walls are in memory of Mr. Russell Wellons. Brother Wellons served on the Holmes Board for many years, and his faithful contributions to the school aided in the Holmes' growth. The Board approved the construction of the Learning Center for classrooms, library, and executive offices. The Board expressed hope that the Fall of 2005 serve as the opening of the new campus. The Ingathering 2004 showered wonderful gifts for the school. Dr. Waters reported nearly $80,000 raised, plus more from the mini-phone-a-thon.[176]

Dr. Waters retired as President of Holmes Bible College in 2008. He served the school for twelve years and witnessed the growth and continual fulfillment of Rev. Holmes' vision for Biblical Education. As the new campus took shape in the vision of the Altamont Missionary and Bible Institute, Dr. Waters' accomplishments found joy and peace in "Well done, good and faithful servant."

Dr. G. Earl Beatty 2008-2009

Upon Dr. Richard Waters' retirement, the Board appointed Dr. G. Earl Beatty as an interim President of Holmes Bible College. His educational accomplishments were Holmes Bible College with a Bachelor of Sacred Literature in 1957, the University of Rio Grande with a B.S.E.E. in 1965, a

Masters of Divinity from Asbury Theological Seminary in 1970, and a Doctor of Ministry from Erskine Theological Seminary in 1987.

Dr. G. Earl and Nancy L. Beatty

His Pastoral experience found him serving congregations in Jackson, Ohio; Bay Minette, Alabama; Lexington, Kentucky and Franklin Springs, Georgia, over twenty-seven years. Dr. Beatty served as a bi-vocational pastor and taught in Pike County Public Schools in Ohio. In 1973, a call from Dr. C. Y. Melton called for his services. His new position at Emmanuel College was Dean of the School of Christian Ministries. His teaching career at Emmanuel listed him as a Professor for Homiletics I and II, Life & Work of the Minister, and the Gospel of John (Inductive Study). Very talented, Beatty's qualifications as a pastor and educator fit nicely with Emmanuel's needs. Before his call as President of Holmes, he served as Dean of the School of Christian Ministries for ten years, Academic Dean for eleven years, and finally, Executive Vice-President of Emmanuel College. As he entered retirement, his desire remained to teach as an Adjunct Professor in Pastoral Theology. Dr. Beatty, an alumnus of Holmes, now entertained a new adventure as the school soon would move to the new campus. As he was given a tour of the new facilities, he said, "I get goosebumps even now thinking of how I felt as I walked into that beautiful edifice that shall soon be the new Holmes Bible College."[177]

President Chris Thompson remembers Dr. Beatty as a great encourager to the faculty and staff. As interim President, he focused on maintaining the vision of the College. This focus centered on excellence in academics, faculty, and students. Until today, his former students remember his Homiletic classes. Dr. Beatty served his Lord and Savior during this interim Presidency to prepare a portrait of the next President as needed. This portrait influenced the choice of Bishop James D. Leggett as the next President. Dr. Beatty continued his service at Holmes for eight years as Academic Dean under President Leggett. Both men were close friends, even as golfing buddies.

Bishop James D. Leggett 2009-2017

Bishop Leggett became the sixth President of Holmes Bible College on October 1, 2009. Bishop Thompson recalls that Holmes stood at a critical point in its history as the campus relocation became a reality. This reality included a new Holmes Memorial Tabernacle Pentecostal Church, the Brooks-King Missions Duplex, the President's Home, and the Ellenberg Student Center needing their final construction and providing plans for the Freeman/Duncan Dormitory for Women. In addition to campus construction, he updated the accounting system for the College with Till and Butler, C.P.A.s, and William C. Cox of Martus Solutions.

Bishop James D. and Faye W. Leggett

Bishop Leggett held a Bachelor of Theology from Holmes Bible College, a Bachelors Degree from the University of North Carolina at Pembroke, and an honorary Doctor of Divinity from Holmes in 1988. His educational achievements prepared him for leadership of the school. Additionally, Dr. Leggett served for twenty-four years in the pastorate of the North Carolina Conference and eventually as the Superintendent of the Conference in 1986. In 1989 he was elected Assistant General Superintendent of the I.P.H.C. His portfolio included the Executive Director of Evangelism U.S.A. and President of the Extension Loan Fund. Three times Bishop Leggett was elected General Superintendent of the I.P.H.C. between August 1997 to July 2009.

In addition, Bishop Leggett served on various national and international committees representing his Lord and the I.P.H.C. He held positions with the Evangelical-Pentecostal Church, co-chair of the Pentecostal/Charismatic Churches of North America, Chairman of the World Pentecostal Conference, the National Association of Evangelicals, the International Charismatic Executive Committee and Religious Alliance Against Pornography. His life achievements provided keen insight into matters of shaping a college and contacts to make Holmes Bible College known throughout the world.

Bishop Leggett taught three classes: Romans, Corinthians, and Spiritual Formation. During his Presidency, he led in signing a new Affiliation with the International Pentecostal Holiness Church. In addition, he pastored Holmes Memorial Church from 2011-2017. He was instrumental in moving the Church from the Briggs Campus to the new campus. Prior to his retirement as President, Bishop Leggett announced at the Alumni Banquet that the college was debt free.[178] On October 4, 2018, the road into the campus was dedicated to Bishop and Mrs. Leggett.

On February 8, 2018, the College received news of the untimely death of former President Leggett. In tribute to him, the College closed classes, and many students and faculty traveled to Falcon, N. C. for his celebration. The College Ensemble dedicated a medley of songs to him.

Bishop Chris Thompson 2017-Present

Rev. D. Chris and Betty R. Thompson

Bishop Chris Thompson became the seventh President of Holmes Bible College in July 2017. He was called in June 2017 to become Pastor of Holmes Memorial Church. Holmes Bible College holds the distinction of three Bishops attending and serving the I.P.H.C. Bishop Thompson received a Bachelor of Theology from Holmes Bible College in 1974 and a B. A. degree from Campbell University in 1977. He joined the N. C. Conference of the Pentecostal Holiness Church in 1971 and received ordination in 1973.

His portfolio is extensive as a Pastor, Instructor at Holmes from 1972-1974 and at Heritage Bible College in Dunn, NC as a New Testament Greek professor. In 1990 he became Director of Evangelism, World Missions, and Archives Director for the N. C. Conference. He planted over 100 churches during his directorship. The N. C. Conference elected Bishop Thompson as its Bishop/Superintendent from 2001-2009. Bishop Thompson served on the Trustees Board of Emmanuel College from 2001-2009. During his tenure as Superintendent/Bishop of the North Carolina Conference, he served as Chairman of the Falcon Children's Home Board in the years 2002-2009. In 2002 he became a Member of the Holmes Bible College Board of Trustees. At the General Conference, he served as the National Executive Director of Evangelism U.S.A. from 2009-2017. He was also the Vice Chairman of the I.P.H.C. During his General Conference service, Bishop Thompson served as the Superintendent of Harvest (Kansas) Conference 2014-2017 and the ACTS Today Conference 2009-2017. Upon completion of his term in 2017 as Bishop of E.V.U.S.A., he became Holmes Bible College President and the Pastor of Holmes Memorial Tabernacle Pentecostal Church from 2017 to the present.

President Thompson's accomplishments for Holmes include the completion of the Ellenberg Student Center, the construction of the Freeman-Duncan Dormitory for Women, The dedication and signage for Leggett Way, the Jack Kelley/George and Nadine Wilson Flagpole Project and Memorial Brick Garden, the construction of the Richard D. and Ella Waters Prayer and Missions Garden, and the Carl. O. Sturkie maintenance facility. His educational promotion of Holmes orchestrated an agreement with Heritage Bible College in Dunn, N. C., where students are able to graduate with an accredited degree. He has reached out to the Church of God of Prophecy, the Congregational Holiness Church, the Church of God, and the Assemblies of God to provide education for their students. A Financial Officer and Office have been established. A Bachelor of Theology for BEAM (Biblical Education for Adults in Ministry) became a reality. President Thompson's vision for Holmes includes extending Holmes' influence around the world. The first extension is in Mexico with the cooperation of Missionary Ron Roy.

President Thompson teaches five classes: Romans, Church Planting and Revitalization, Senior Seminar, Personal Money Management, and Spiritual Formation each semester. During his tenure, he also serves as the Academic Dean of the College. Plans are being formulated for a Music Minor. For college support, a "Sustainer Program" for Donors now functions to aid students and budget. With his wife, Mrs. Betty Thompson, an Archives

Department has been established. President Thompson authorized and produced this book, *A History of Holmes Bible College*, authored by Dr. Stan York.

President Thompson's gifts and graces have provided a steady sailing ship even during the Covid times and the cultural turmoil today. His vision for Holmes Bible College pursues the original goal of Reverend N. J. Holmes, to train pastors, teachers, and missionaries to spread the Gospel in the world. As he graduated in 1974, he heard the Lord speak clearly, "You will return!"

Sister Nina

Nina C. Holmes

In church life or Christian school history, it is easy to remember the great men and their leadership, but a story remains for great women as additions to the story. Sister Nina belongs in the history of Holmes Bible College. As male leadership is viewed as loud and demanding, the same could be said of female leadership. Yet the lasting leadership impressions establish historical markers of endurance and faithfulness. These leaders know the value of "be still and know that I am God."

Sister Nina Cotton Holmes was born on February 5, 1885. Desirous of strengthening her relationship with Jesus and discerning His Will for her, Sister Nina arrived on Paris Mountain in 1909. At the Institute, she became a lifelong learner and disciple of Jesus. There she met Zelotes Lee Holmes, Rev. N. J. Holmes' nephew, and they married in a double wedding with Rev. Paul F. Beacham and Miss Nell Lane as the first weddings in the Tabernacle in Greenville. Zelotes was chosen to follow Rev. Holmes as the leader of the Institute, but he passed away two years after their wedding. Yet Sister Nina was firm in her conviction to assist Rev. N. J. and Sister Lucy Holmes in any way possible. Prior to her marriage, she worked on many summer camp meetings and evangelistic tours with the Holmes.

As God directed Sister Nina's life, her love for the school led her to Briggs Avenue, the new campus. Her service for the school allowed her to serve as Registrar, Dean of Girls, Dietician, Music teacher, and Librarian, yet her greatest role was as a mentor for future lady ministers, missionaries, pastors' wives, and disciples of Jesus. In 1926, G. F. Taylor began his studies at the University of North Carolina, and Mrs. Nina assumed responsibility for the Missions Column in *The Advocate*. She lived in an apartment above the school office in the "White House." Female students, over the years, anxiously awaited an invitation to the Saturday meal.

Her service continued in the Holmes Memorial Church as Song leader, Choir Director, and Sunday School teacher. She organized the Ladies' Aid group for female students. One recalled her devotion to Bible Study as she faithfully attended Bible classes for as long as she could go. K. A. Carlisle writing in *The Co-Worker* for the Western Conference of North Carolina, recalled, "However, since Mrs. Holmes has touched so many students' lives that are a part of this conference and contributed toward making them better and more effective servants of the Lord and the Church...we think it quite fitting that this issue of *The Co-Worker* be dedicated to her."[179]

After serving Jesus and his fellow believers for over fifty years, Mrs. Nina entered her heavenly home in 1976. Her witness and lessons continue to this day.

4. Voices of Holmes—Past and Present

The Voices of Holmes chapter represents letters and testimonies reported in articles both past and present. This chapter provides important testimony of the power, presence, and purity in Holmes' training for men and women since 1898. In addition to the testimonies, several articles from *The Holmes Bible College Bulletin* and *The Voice of Holmes* provide information on former Holmes students and their further education and ministries. An attentive ear will discover God's Hand in the school's founding and maintaining a positive Holiness/Pentecostal witness in this world. Please remember, Christians are built-up with the testimonies of the saints!

*****

A card received from our sister, Miss Olive May, tells us that the Lord is opening the way for her to leave for China January 1 in company with Miss Mary Duncan of N.C. She is one of our students and we know the prayers of the Institute will follow her.

The Altamont Witness Volume 1 Number 2 Miss Olive May

Brother Amos Bradley, wife, and baby, Missionaries from Central America are now with us. He expects to leave for work in Southern Alabama. Mrs. Bradley will remain with us through the closing exercises of the school. At a good service last night, the 14th Bro. Bradley gave a forcible message on the need of workers in the foreign fields—which we felt reached some hearts.

The Altamont Witness Volume 1 Number 3

The name Altamont is still sweet to us, because we often met God in a precious way while there. It has surely been a coaling station to us, and a place of deeper crucifixion to self, and the obtaining of a richer life in God. How glad we are that God ever led us that way, to store up some truths that we are now giving out to the people.

The Altamont Witness Volume 1 Number 11. J. E. Boehmer

I praise God for leading me by the way of Altamont and for the precious lessons learned there and the deep truths learned there that are hid away in the Word, which have proven a great blessing to me in the work he has called me to do…And here I want to thank Bro. and Sister Holmes for their kindness to me while at Altamont.

The Altamont Witness Volume 1 Number 12. Mrs. Lorena Cotton

I want to praise the dear Lord this afternoon for the privilege of spending two terms and one vacation at Altamont. I am now starting in another term of school. I have been trusting the Lord for my needs during this time, and He has not failed me one time, for which we praise Him.

The Altamont Witness Volume 2 Number 12 T.A. Melton (A Director of Foreign Missions for the Pentecostal Holiness Church, former Superintendent of the Western Conference of the PHC, and Superintendent on the national level)

Then He spoke to me about helping others, and of course that looked impossible, for I have been a working girl, and little opportunity to attend school. But I learned of a school near Greenville, S.C. for those who wanted to do Christian work, and God led me this way. After coming I began to see the need of a clean heart, and two weeks later the Lord wonderfully sanctified me…But this is not all, for on December 25, 1907, the Lord baptized me with the Holy Ghost…I must not stop without praising God for Altamont, for eternity alone will the blessing it has been to me.

The Altamont Witness Volume 2 Number 19 Sallie Brigman

I am glad to let the Readers of the Witness know that I am here at the Institute for the opening of another term of school. This is one of the most precious places on earth to me. There is no place, that I know of, where the Bible is taught and practiced as here.

The Altamont Witness Volume 4 Number 14 W. H. Turner (Missionary to China, Head of Missions for the PHC, Church Evangelist)

We spent several seasons at Dr. N. J. Holmes Bible School at Greenville, S. C. and are now in evangelistic work. The Lord brought me from Poland to Germany, and from Germany to London, and from London to New York and from New York to Greenville, S.C. to hear Christ preached in his fullness. I hope whoever reads this may think of Jesus who did so much for me.

The Altamont Witness Volume 6 Number 13 Lewis Sawgalsky

I want to praise God for the blessed privilege of being back in school at the beginning of another term. Jesus has been precious to me during the vacation months, and has brought me back with a determination to study, work, and pray, getting ready to work for the master...I praise God for this Institution, where we students can come and have such consecrated teachers. They are giving their lives for this work. Eternity will only reveal what dear Bro. and Sister Holmes have done and are doing for this world.

The Altamont Witness Volume 6 Number 18 Julia Payne (Missionary to China)

I am glad to be in school again, and I praise God for His faithfulness to me even when I have been so unfaithful. From my early childhood there has been an earnest desire in my heart to be wholly given to God. At the age of twelve I was saved and sanctified, and later received the Baptism of the Holy Spirit, but through disobedience I lost victory, and soon backslid...As we begin the Bible class one afternoon last week, we all were made to rejoice when God took charge of things, and gave us a lesson. He was present in healing and Baptising (sic) power, and I am glad to say that at that time I received the Holy Spirit.

The Altamont Witness Volume 6 Number 20 Mary Wilkes Andrews (Missionary to China)

We are glad to learn of the steady progress made in the study of language by our beloved Brother Byus in India. Brother Byus is one of our newest missionaries, and it is encouraging to know that he is getting along so well.

Brothers J. A. Killebrew, H. B. Johnson and H. A. Brooks have united their efforts in evangelistic work for the summer. They have conducted meetings in North Carolina, and the first two named are at this writing conducting a tent meeting in Portsmouth, VA for Brother H. T. Spence.

The Herald of Truth, Introductory Issue 1927.

Brother and Sister J. W. Warren will be in Oklahoma, the native state of Mr. Warren, by the time this reaches the public. Since June 1 Mr. and Mrs. Warren have been almost incessantly engaged in evangelistic work in the South. During this time they have done untold good and have made many lasting friends. They expect to remain in Oklahoma until early spring when they will return East to make preparations to sail for Africa, their chosen field of labor.

Miss Verdie Johnson, our newest missionary to Africa, is residing in the home of Brother and Sister D. D. Freeman. It is reported that Sister Johnson is making steady progress in the study of the language and is happy in her work.

By the time this issue of the HERALD reaches our readers, Rev. and Mrs. T. H. Rousseau and family will have sailed for China where they will resume their work as missionaries. November 22 is the date for sailing. Brother and Sister Rousseau will relieve Brother and Sister W. H. Turner who will come to America on a furlough. Their homecoming is made necessary by the declining health of Mrs. Turner.

Herald of Truth December 12, 1927

Rev. M. E. Parrish writes us from India that he is making good progress in his studies. He has already passed the examination on first year Hindi, in less than ten months: and he expects to finish the second year by the fall of 1928. After that time, Brother Parrish will be engaged in active service as a missionary.

Herald of Truth January 1, 1928

Miss Florence C. Hamilton is teaching in the Bible School in British Columbia which had its initial beginning this Fall…Miss Hamilton was quite an asset to Holmes, and we know she will be an efficient teacher as well as an enthusiastic promoter of missions wherever she serves.

Rev. Edwin Ditto heads a Sharon Bible School in California for the second term. Rev. and Mrs. Elmer Rouse are on the teaching staff.

The Holmes Bible College Bulletin November 1945

Rev. A. M. Herndon is entering upon his third year as pastor of the First Pentecostal Holiness Church in Memphis, Tenn. Mrs. A. M. Herndon is assisting her husband in his ministry by her good gospel singing which is an asset to the work. She is also a member of the Official Board of The Women's Auxiliary of the Tri-State Conference.

Rev. G. A. Byus (Missionary to India) is pastoring the Tacoma, Wash. P. H. Church. He writes, "God not only laid this great North Western Territory on our hearts, but opened the Way for us to enter and to become settled where we can go forward with the task He gave us."

The Holmes Bible College Bulletin December 1945

From South Africa, Rev. and Mrs. D. D. Freeman report a good conference at Pretoria under the leadership of Rev. Alpheus Noseworthy who has sailed to America.

The Voice of Holmes May 1947

Rev. John B. Parker is pastoring the Bethel P. H. Church, Bethel, N. C. for the second consecutive year, while he continues his studies at the East Carolina Teachers College.

Rev. and Mrs. Jimmie Jordan are teaching at Sharon Bible School, Maderia, California. Mr. Jordan is Dean of the boys.

Miss Dot Woodson is a Junior at Furman University.

Rev. and Mrs. S. J. Todd are pastoring the First Pentecostal Holiness Church of Memphis, Tenn.

The Voice of Holmes November 1948

The Lord has given us fine opportunities this past year—doors have been opened of our own, all free of debt for which we greatly praise God...I am leaving at daybreak up the river to the hills. It may be the last time we can go, as the country all around is over run with Communists, waiting to take over the cities if the government collapses—China certainly needs our prayers.

The Voice of Holmes January 1949 Florence O. Hamilton

As for the work that we are doing, it is going fine. In fact, I never dreamed of our being able to accomplish so much here, but God certainly opened the doors wide for the Gospel in Brazil. There is some persecution, but for the most part we are treated well here. I was stoned a couple times, and have been called almost every ugly name under the sun, but what it this in comparison with gaining souls and planting the Word in needy places.

The Voice of Holmes January 1949 Chester Miller

An extended education, a "good time," and hope for the future: all colleges bestow these qualities. However, even more valuable achievements are accomplished at Holmes.

Through true discipleship to Jesus, I can earn an education that the world can neither give nor take away. The fact that Holmes is a faith school gives me a true sense of dependence on Him. What better way to learn and survive at the same time than to put out trust in God.

Surely, all colleges claim to have a "good time" in their learning techniques and academics, but how many can actually profess "best times"? None, but Holmes. For my college is in tune with the very creator of "time" itself.

Most of all Holmes College of the Bible prepares me for the future that most schools know little of. This future is eternity. Let the world have the near future, but let the prepared have eternity.

For these reasons, Holmes means more than any other college could mean. I choose to live by Luke 12:33 and lay my treasures in a heaven that "faileth not, where no thief approacheth, and no moth corrupteth." Holmes teaches me what those treasures are.

Voice of Holmes Fall 1981 Donna Gardner

A Spiritual Time-Piece

Having served on the faculty of Holmes for nine years I have been able to observe the working of the hand of God here in a special way. What makes Holmes tick? Actually, there are several things. The college could well be likened to a clock—for we strive to make every moment count: we are held in God's hand: as for the winding of the clock, it comes from the Lord Himself as faithful friends pray for and support the institution. He has abundantly answered prayers, enabling Holmes to tick off over ninety years of faithful service, and to count hundreds of young lives which have been fitted to His Timetable. Holmes is a spiritual time-piece. Unique. Faithful. Needful of your assistance.

There is no student at Holmes who is not special to us. One of the joys of working here is to see each individual student, with his own unique background and potential for the Lord, grow and mature as an effective Christian servant. Holmes is a proven consistent builder of church leaders, ministers, and laymen, but I, as a faculty member, have learned many things and valuable lessons from the students.

It is also a joy to observe and work with the other faculty and staff members here. They exhibit so many Christian qualities that are sometimes unseen by the public eye. They truly have eternity in their hearts. Their willingness to sacrifice and serve in love and grace is one of the components that prevents this Christian institution from deteriorating into mere academics and form. I thank God for Holmes and its ministry.

Voice of Holmes Fall 1988 Joe McKinney

Rodney Bohler ('84) missionary to the Crow Indians, called from Hardin, Montana. Bohler is a minister with the Pentecostal Church of God and he and his wife have three sons...Bohler said, "Holmes took me in, loved me, trained me, and gave me a foundation for ministry that I am still building upon.H" e briefly described his work on the Crow Indian Reservation and related some of the struggles and also the victories that have come as he and his family have ministered among that tribe."

Holmes Magazine Winter 1998 Volume 3 Number 1, page 4.

I have been at Holmes only a short time but I can already testify of the transforming work God is doing in my life. God is using the teachers of the Bible classes to help me gain a better understanding and hunger for His Word. I am amazed at the changes God is doing in my life and in the lives of my fellow students.

I wish I could find the words to express my gratitude to all the friends who support Holmes Bible College. Thank you for allowing me to be here and for being a vital part of my Christian education.

Holmes Magazine May 2000 Volume 5 Number 1, page 3. Avril Fortuin

I have had quite an experience at Holmes, I have met a lot of people, but especially I have built a lot of relationships with other students that I will never forget. This place has really taught me how to live for others. We have excellent teachers who know how to discipline us and we have fun learning under them at the same time. It will really mean a lot to the students to move to a new campus. We will be able to learn in a better environment. And problems with the classrooms being flooded will be solved. It will really be great. - Vivian Ige from Nigeria

I love Holmes Bible College. I enjoy all of my classes. My teachers are all wonderful and I am always blessed in the chapel services. I am thankful for this college. I am so excited about the new campus that will be built. I look forward to the future and all the wonderful things that are in store for the school. - Doranden Atkins

Holmes Magazine Fall 2004 Volume 9 Number 1, pgs. 1 & 4.

For more than a century, Holmes Bible College has stood like a beacon for Christians in the Holiness/Pentecostal tradition. As the oldest continuing Pentecostal college in the world, Holmes has educated several generations of Pentecostal pastors and lay leaders for the Body of Christ. The faculty has maintained a wonderful balance and integrity in holding firmly to the timeless truths of the Bible while moving confidently to face the challenges of the future. I highly recommend Holmes as a wonderful Bible college for future pastors and church leaders.

A *View of Holmes Bible College 2010* Dr. Vinson Synan

The rapid pace of change in today's world calls for followers of Christ to adapt to these changes while remaining anchored to Christ and His Word. The study of God's Word is most effective when it is applied to service in the real world. This is the vision of Holmes Bible College. It is a joy to recommend the programs of Holmes for any who desire to prepare for ministry or who simply want to be better equipped as a disciple of Jesus Christ.

Dr. Elaine Vaden, Class of 1965, Valedictorian

A Biblically based ministry focus for tomorrow is yours today at Holmes Bible College as you study under Holy Spirit anointed leaders who understand relevance with scriptural compromise.

Rev. T. Elwood Long Holmes alumnus

Holmes Bible College is a place we were so honored to call home for 4 years. We learned so much about God and His Word, but also about the ministry. Holmes is a place of preparation. With the education that we received from the amazing teachers there, we were prepared when difficult situations came up in the ministry, and also when those difficult questions came. We are so thankful for the ministry of Holmes Bible College, and we are thankful that even though we are no longer students there, that we can still call it home.

Rev. Zachary L. and Hannah Tomlinson, Class 2020, 2022

I am so grateful to Holmes Bible College, for being given the privilege to be part of this family of God-loving people who are selfishly and extraordinarily devoted to provide ministerial and biblical training to men and women who love the Lord and are on fire to serve Him. Holmes has an important role to play in shaping one's personality and foundation of Scripture, God, and His church. In many ways, I am who I am today because of this school. My heart is filled with immense pride, fondness, gratitude and nostalgia of this school. As I graduate, I walk away from here with more than just lessons learned about the Bible or church administration; I walk away with the advice, thought, and prayers of those who educated me, and for that I will be forever grateful. I am convinced that what makes this college special is the professors and staff who selfishly and humbly give without measure and are willing to do anything they can, to make each student success in all aspects of life. They demonstrate what it means to be passionate about a subject, God's people, and His Word, while pouring love and wisdom into their students and serving Christ in everything they do in and out of the classroom. Holmes will forever be in my thoughts and prayers, and I wish one day to be able to repay and support the college that gave me everything I needed, to help me succeed in accomplishing God's calling for my life. There's truly no place like Holmes.

Camila Villanueva S. International Student, Santiago, Chile, 2018-2023

Dear reader, my name is Madison Smith, and I came to Holmes Bible College in the fall of 2019. It was one of the best decisions of my life. Holmes has not only shaped me and taught me more about God's Word, but it has given me rich experiences in ministry, and sweet memories. I have seen God's hand at work in my life these four years, and I have made lifelong friends.

Holmes has been like a sunrise after a long night in my life. I never dreamed I would meet such wonderful people that I have been blessed to call family. I have learned so much during my time here. When I came to the college, I thought I had a great deal of knowledge already, however, the more I learned in the classrooms, the more I realized that I really didn't know much.

Holmes Bible College has taught me that I am not alone in life. Holmes has taught me the importance of dividing the Word of truth rightly. It has taught me that the world doesn't revolve around me, and that I should do my best to have an outward focus, rather than an inward focus. Holmes has taught me to love others, and to live for others. My time at the school has shown me that I AM a leader, and I have impact. I have the ability to affect change.

Holmes has given me a new perspective. As I have seen all of the different cultures and countries represented here at the school come together, I have marveled at the beauty of all of our differences. The only thing that joins most of us together and causes us to run in the same crowd is Jesus and the price He paid.

The school is a wonderful haven in a dark world. It's not perfect, but it's priceless. Here I have witnessed the sweet tears of my friends as they labored in prayer. Here I have had good days, and bad days. Here I have heard the precious Word of God preached. Here I have praised and sang worship to the King of Kings with some of the best people on earth. Here I have experienced tears of joy, and tears of pain, endured arguments, and made up again, thought about giving up, yet pressed on again, been frustrated with the Bible, yet chosen to keep seeking understanding. Here on this campus many times I have poured my heart out to God, and I know He heard me. Here on this campus I have studied, laughed, cried, shared meals with friends, served, and preached. But most importantly, here I have felt the presence of God.

May God continue to bless Holmes and the people who are a part of it, in any and every capacity. May He use us to further His kingdom and His will. May He guide us and show us His love, always leading us beside still waters, and into green pastures. May Holmes continue to be a place where people find rest, acceptance, and family, and may God send us out into all the earth to complete His purposes. May we see miracles and answered prayers and come back to these hallowed grounds to tell others of what God has done.

Madison Smith, Class of 2023

I was called to preach during my Junior year at the University of North Carolina at Charlotte. My major was business administration and my goals were primarily financially focused. I believed it to be God's will to complete that degree program since I had already invested that much time, money, and energy into it. There was, however, no doubt in my mind that Holmes Theological Seminary, as it was then called, was the place where God wanted to change the direction and focus of my life.

The three year program of practical and theological training and preparation was literally transformational. It brought to fruition in my life what it means to be "transformed by the renewing of your mind so that you may prove what is that good and acceptable and perfect will of God." The Bible focus was intensive, two hours a day, supplemented with classes in theology, apologetics, philosophy and a list of practical application courses to round it all out.

Holmes was amazing! It wasn't only about educating my mind, but about transforming my life. We were taught by Word and Deed to live by faith, to live for others, and to live for God. Those lessons, forty-six years later, continue to shape my life and ministry. I am forever grateful!

Darrell Greene, Pastor of North Pointe IPHC, Holmes Alumnus, Executive Board of Cornerstone Conference, and Executive Board of Holmes Bible College.

5. The Seven Pillars of Education at Holmes Bible College

Pillar One-President N. J. Holmes (1898-1919)

"The purpose of the school from the very beginning has been to serve men and women of all denominations who are called to the ministry. We believe that the development of the highest type of Christian character and the helping of those who are to enter Christian service to understand sufficiently and to rightly interpret and consistently apply the Word of God. We commit with confidence and faith, the entire Bible and Missionary Institute to Christ, the great Head of the Church, trusting that the government shall be upon His shoulders, praying that it may ever be under the good providence of God, who knows the past, surveys the future, and supplies the needs of His people."

Pillar Two-President Paul F. Beacham (1919-1978)

"Any school that does not turn out a moral product that will be as a light to illuminate and salt to penetrate and preserve the soundness of society is woefully failing in its purpose. The person who is intellectual but not deep enough to be honest in the fear of God is a menace to society. When the Christian viewpoint is lost in education, the way is opened for the development and progress of the destructive forces that are always just as active as they are permitted to be. True education does not put too much faith in mere knowledge. It is my conviction that Holmes Theological Seminary can be counted upon to preserve and pass on to others those lofty principles that make purity and right the real objective in education, than the mere acquirement of knowledge."

Pillar Three-President Kenneth D. Benson (1978-1996)

"Holmes is an educational opportunity for the serious-minded, sober, and mature Christian who has a special consciousness of God's calling upon his or her life. Our constant effort will be to develop a deep, sober, spiritual life, to engender a lifelong spirit of prayer and a passion for the salvation of souls. Holmes regards the Bible as its chief knowledge and the supreme source of its message. The Bible is taken as the highest standard of mental accuracy, imparting an intellectual vigor that nothing but contact with the Divine mind can give. The old should not be thrown aside merely because it is old. 'Thus, saith the Lord,' is still the ultimate criterion of truth and righteousness at Holmes College of the Bible."

Pillar Four-President Richard Waters (1996-2008)

"When I think of education as it relates to Holmes Bible College, my thoughts are immediately drawn to the great Apostle Paul's statement to Timothy, 'Be diligent to present yourself to God as a workman who does not need to be ashamed handling the word of truth' 2 Timothy 2:15 (NASB). In 1898 Holmes Bible College was established to educate, equip, and prepare men and women to fulfill various forms of Christian ministry. It was my goal that Holmes Bible College should become the very best among colleges to prepare its students for Christian ministry. I was tremendously pleased when I received a letter from Erskine College informing me that Holmes Bible College students were the best prepared for graduate studies of all students they accepted from other colleges. This letter also commends the preparedness of the faculty and staff. To God be all the glory."

Pillar Five-President G. Earl Beatty (2008-2009)

"Having spent twenty-three years being educated and thirty-six years as an educator, I have learned two basic outcomes. One may be educated for professional purposes to make a living, and /or one may be educated to make a life. Both offer degrees. Holmes Bible College seeks to prepare one to make a life. As opposed to being served, Holmes graduates seek to serve. Biblical thinking cannot be achieved with intensive study of God's Word. The world is the limit of such an educational outcome. On the other hand, one educated for a profession limits one's expectations to the highest salary or the enhancement of one's prestige. The difference answers the question: 'Do I just make a living, or do I want to invest in lives?' The answer is spelled out at Holmes Bible College."

Pillar Six-President James D. Leggett (2009-2017)

"The core of the curriculum at Holmes Bible College is the Word of God. The students are challenged to study the Word so that they can rightly divide it. The purpose is to instill in their hearts a love for the truth of God's Word as a guide to them for their lives and ministries. 'Go into the world and preach the Gospel to every creature' (Mark 16:15). The preaching of the Word as His witnesses requires courage. The word 'witness' is the root of martyrs. Nevertheless, it does not matter the cost. Our mission at Holmes Bible College is to proclaim that Word to the ends of the earth."

Pillar Seven-President D. Chris Thompson (2017-Present)

"Holmes Bible College exists to build the Kingdom of God by adding more and equipping the members to be fully equipped. My favorite verses in thinking of Holmes are Ephesians 4:11-12. They read as follows: 'And He Himself gave some to be apostles, some prophets and teachers, for the equipping of the saints for the work of the ministry, for the edifying of the body of Christ.' The Lord brings to us these future gifts and/or leaders for His body. Holmes' job is to place the joints in place, to make the frame functional, to clean and mend these lifesaving nets, and to place the pieces into His puzzle. What a job it is! Our job of Biblical education is absolutely essential to the expansion and growth of His body. To know the Word of God is to know the plans of Creator God. Without Him, we can do nothing! 'But they that do know their God, shall be strong and shall do exploits in His Name'" (Daniel 11:32).

Appendices

Holmes Bible College Board of Trustees 2023-2024

Rev. W.A. Mills, Chairman, Colfax, NC

Rev. Jewelle Stewart, Vice-Chairman, Effingham, SC

Rev. Darrell Green, Secretary, Kernersville, NC

Dr. Eddie Allen, Treasurer, Mauldin, SC

Bishop Ray Boggs, Greenwood, SC

Dr. John Hedgepeth, Fayetteville, NC

Pastor Hasker Hudgens, Greenville, SC

Rev. Janice Marshburn, Jacksonville, NC

Bishop Preston Mathena, Dublin, VA

Bishop Tommy McGhee, ex officio *(seat & voice)*, Oklahoma City, OK

Bishop Danny Nelson, Falcon, NC

Rev. Bill Rose, Goldsboro, NC

Mr. Garland Slate, Fayetteville, NC

Bishop Morris Smith, Florence, SC

Mr. Michael Sturkie, Lexington, SC

Rev. D. Chris Thompson, ex officio member, Greenville, SC

Bishop Jeffrey White, Elizabethtown, KY

Personnel of Holmes Bible College

(Full Time and Part Time) 2023

Staff

D. Chris Thompson, President, Dean of Academics

- M.Min. - Southwestern Christian University
- B.A. – Campbell University
- Th. B - Holmes Bible College
- North Carolina State University
- Church Growth Associate – Monrovia, CA
- Dynamic Church Planting International, Sr. Master Trainer
- Ordained, International Pentecostal Holiness Church

Barbara A. Bishop, Registrar/Immigration Officer

- B.S.L. – Holmes Bible College
- University of V.A. – Continuing Ed.
- Dublin Community College – Sheriff's Office Training Course

K. Bruce Hagee, Director of Student Life

- B.A.– Holmes Bible College
- Ordained, International Pentecostal Holiness Church

Jacquelyn J. Rhodes, Business/Finance/President's Executive Assistant

- B.S. – Holmes Bible College

Wanda Bucklew, Dietician/Social Director/Procurement Officer

- ServeSafe® Certified Manager/Dietician

Hannah Tomlinson, Admissions Officer/Receptionist

- B.S. – Holmes Bible College
- Ordained, International Pentecostal Holiness Church

Naomi Huff, Residence Director of Women/Chapel Worship Leader

- Christ Central Institute
- Holmes Bible College
- Ordained, International Pentecostal Holiness Church

K. Dale Huff, Residence Director of Men

- Christ Central Institute
- Holmes Bible College
- Ordained, International Pentecostal Holiness Church

Betty R. Thompson, Archivist

- B.S.L. – Holmes Bible College
- A.A. – Emmanuel College

Nora Freeman, Licensed Professional Counselor

- M.A. - Pentecostal Theological Seminary
- B.S. - Holmes Bible College

D. Jill Hagee, Prayer Coordinator

- Holmes Bible College

President's Council

D. Chris Thompson, Chairman

Members
- Barbara A. Bishop
- Wanda Bucklew
- K. Bruce Hagee
- Jacquelyn J. Rhodes

Faculty

Charles E. Allen, Practical Ministry
- D. Min. – Erskine Theological Seminary
- M.A. – Pentecostal Theological Seminary
- B.S. - University of South Carolina
- A.A. Anderson University
- Ordained, Church of God

Donald Auwarter, Music
- Bob Jones University

Ronnie W. Barnes, Missions
- M.A. – Advantage College
- B.A. – Holmes Bible College
- Ordained, International Pentecostal Holiness Church

Carol A. Bush, Library Coordinator
- M.S.L.S. – East Carolina University
- B.S. – East Carolina University

Olga Acosta Clement, Spanish

- B.S. - Holmes Bible College
- B.S. – Universidad Del Atlantico

Paul Evans, Online Instructor

- M.A. – Global University
- B.A. – Holmes Bible College
- A.A. – United Kingdom
- Ordained, International Pentecostal Holiness Church

V. Lamont Freeman, Director of B.E.A.M., Bible, Theology

- D. Min. (Honorary) Covenant Seminary
- M. Div. – Pentecostal Theological Seminary
- B.S. – Holmes Bible College
- Ordained, Church of God

Kristian Kilgore, Bible, Practical Ministry

- M.A.T.S. – Liberty University
- B.A. – Lee University
- Ordained, Church of God

Wilson Kilgore, Christian Ministry, Bible, Theology

- M. Min. – Pentecostal Theological Seminary
- B.S. – Lee University
- Ordained, Church of God

Brent Lollis, B.E.A.M. Instructor

- D. Min. – Covington Theological Seminary
- M. Min. – Southwestern Christian University
- B.A. – Clemson University
- Ordained, International Pentecostal Holiness Church

Joe L. McKinney, Theology, Greek

- M.A. – Bob Jones University
- B.A. Southern Wesleyan University
- Th.B. – Holmes Bible College

M. Dean Morgan, Online Instructor

- M.A. – Asbury Theological Seminary
- B.A. – Central Wesleyan College
- Th.B. – Holmes Bible College
- Ordained, International Pentecostal Holiness Church

John Petty, Online Instructor

- M.A.A. – Luther Rice University
- B.S. – Holmes Bible College
- A.A. – Holmes Bible College
- Ordained, Church of God

Steve Shealy, Bible, General Instruction

- M. A.T.S. – Erskine Theological Seminary
- Th.B. – Holmes Bible College

D. Chris Thompson, Bible, Practical Ministry

- *(see above)*

Matthew Turner, Online Instructor

- D.Min. – South University
- M.A. – Liberty University
- B.A. – Jacksonville State University
- Ordained, Congregational Holiness Church

Stacy Watford, Director of Online, Instructor

- M.A. - Erskine Theological Seminary
- B.S. – Holmes Bible College
- Ordained, Church of God

Carol Watson, Advisor - Music

- M.A. – Furman University
- B.A. - Central Wesleyan College
- B.S.L. – Holmes Bible College

David Wheeler, Online Instructor

- M.A. – East Carolina University
- B.A. – University of North Carolina
- A.A. – Florida Community College
- Ordained, International Pentecostal Holiness Church

Donald Woodward, General Instruction

- Th.D – Masters Int. Univ. of Divinity
- D.PT – Masters Int. Univ. of Divinity
- M.Ed. – Converse University
- M.A. – Ashland Theological Seminary
- B.A. – Southern Wesleyan University
- Th .B – Holmes Theological Seminary

Programs of Study

Certificate for Bible and Related Studies

The Christian Ministries Certificate Program is a two-year special studies program for students who do not aspire or feel inclined to pursue a degree from Holmes Bible College.

Requirements for the Certificate:

- The student must observe Catalog rules for class attendance.

- If desired, a student may take one semester's work toward a degree before applying for the concentration of study for a Certificate. All courses taken during that semester will apply toward the academic requirements of the Certificate whether or not the student made passing grades.

- No tests are required, but individual instructors may assign readings and written projects as requirements. No numerical or letter grading is given, and all courses are Pass-Fail.

- Outside observation learning opportunities may be assigned for non-Biblical courses.

- Certificates are awarded at graduation, so students are required to be in attendance.

- Tuition for the program is based on the audit scale as specified in the Catalog. In addition, a full-time student pays the regular general fee.

- The student who stays in the residence hall pays the regular room and board fee provided he/she shall be enrolled in the minimum twelve hours.

- Work-study criteria are applicable to Certificate students.

- The student will pay one-half the graduation fee of a regular degree candidate.

- Refund of the tuition fee is based on the normal refund schedule stipulated on page 14 of the Catalog.

- Rules of residence apply equally to all full-time students, whether Degree or Certificate.

- Students are required to apply for this special program of study completing a form prepared by the Vice-President for Academic Development.
- Vice-President for Academic Development is the advisor for all applicants.

Suggested courses for the program:

YEAR ONE: (28 audit hrs./448 clock hrs.)

Fall Semester

- English 101 or 099
- BIB 101 Old Testament Survey
- MUS 202 Practical Music Skills
- SFD 208 Spiritual Formation
- OLD 402 Poetic and Wisdom Literature
- Chapel

Spring Semester

- BIB 102 New Testament Survey
- FIN 102 Personal Money Management
- BIB 204 Gospel of John **or** Life of Christ
- SFD 208 Spiritual Formation
- THE 302 Pent. Hist. and Theology
- Chapel

YEAR TWO (28 audit hrs./448 clock hrs.)

Fall Semester

- MIN 301 Homiletics I
- NEW 313 Prison and Pastoral Epistles
- OLD 301 Major **or** Minor Prophets
- SFD 208 Spiritual Formation
- NEW 401 Romans and Galatians
- Chapel

Spring Semester

- OLD 302 Historical Books
- NEW 402 I and II Corinthians
- OLD 202 Pentateuch
- SFD 208 Spiritual Formation
- NEW 302 Acts of the Apostles
- Chapel

Associate Degree Program

Holmes Bible College offers one Associate of Arts degree program in Christian Ministry.

The general education courses are taught from a Christian perspective, and the content is specifically structured for ministers in training. Holmes offers a four-dimensional approach to ministerial education – Christian service, Bible and Theology, general education, and practical ministry. This approach enables students to comprehend the truth, understand the world around them, and bridge the gap between the two by acquiring effective ministry techniques.

Requirements for the Associate of Arts (A.A.) Degree

DEGREE REQUIREMENTS   65 credit hours/1072 clock hours

GENERAL STUDIES   24 credit hours/432 clock hours

ENG 101	English Composition I
ENG 102	English Composition II
MIN 301	Homiletics
FIN 102	Personal Money Management

Choose any three of the following:

HIS 101	Western Civilization I or HIS 102 Western Civilization II
GEO 101	World Geography
GOV 102	American Government

SOC 102	General Sociology
CEY 201	Courtship, Marriage and Family
PSY 102	Intro. To Psychology

Choose one of the following:

MUS 201	Practical Music Skills
MUS 202	Music Appreciation
DRM 202	Drama

PRACTICAL   5 credit hours/

SFD 208	Spiritual Formation
PRM 428	Internship
Chapel	

PASTORAL FOUNDATION STUDIES
9 credit hours/208 clock hours

BIB 101	Old Testament Survey
BIB 102	New Testament Survey
MIN 201	Life and Work of the Minister **or**
BIB 203	Hermeneutics

BIBLE
15 credit hours/240clock hours

Old Testament (Choose two):

OLD 202	Pentateuch
OLD 302	Historical Books
OLD 301	Major Prophets or OLD 303 Minor Prophets
OLD 401	Poetic and Wisdom Literature
OLD 402	Daniel and Revelation

New Testament:

NEW 202   Life of Christ

Choose two from the following courses:

NEW 302   Acts of the Apostles

NEW 401   Romans and Galatians

NEW 303   General Epistles

NEW 313   Prison and Pastoral Epistles

NEW 402   I and II Corinthians

THEOLOGY
12 credit hours/192 clock hours

choose four from the following courses:

THE 201   Christian Theology I

THE 202   Christian Theology II

THE 301   Christian Ethics

THE 302   Pentecostal History and Theology

HIS 302   Church History

THE 401   Apologetics

Bachelor Degree Programs

Holmes Bible College offers two bachelor degree programs – Bible and Theology and Christian Ministry. The former program is designed for those desiring seminary training, those who wish to pursue a career in Bible teaching, and those who wish to make preaching the primary focus of their ministry. The latter program offers a multidisciplinary approach to ministry. A Christian Ministry major takes a series of courses from each department of Holmes and concentrates in a minor area tailored to meet individual goals. The major is designed for those wishing to enter the ministry directly upon leaving Holmes.

Both of the bachelor degree programs at Holmes Bible College are premised upon a two-year core academic program of Bible, theology, and general education courses. The general education courses are taught from a Christian perspective, and the content is specifically structured for ministers in training. Holmes offers a four-dimensional approach to ministerial education – Christian service, Bible and theology, general education, and practical ministry. This approach enables the students to comprehend the truth, understand the world around them, and bridge the gap between the two by acquiring effective ministry techniques.

*Prerequisites

- BIB 101 is a prerequisite for all Old Testament courses.
- BIB 102 is a prerequisite for all New Testament Courses.
- ENG 101 is a prerequisite for ENG 102.
- ENG 101 and ENG 102 are prerequisites for ENG 402.
- All foreign language courses must be taken in order from Elementary to Intermediate.
- MIN 301 is a prerequisite for MIN 302.

Degree Requirements
124 credit hours/2160 clock hours

General Education Requirements
37 credit hrs./624 clock hrs.

English and Communication

9 credit hours/144 clock hrs.

ENG 101	English Composition I
ENG 102	English Composition II
ENG 402	Survey of Literature

Math and Science   4 credit hrs./96 clock hrs.

Freshman Orientation

FIN 102	Personal Money Management

Social Sciences   15 credit hrs. /240 clock hrs.

HIS 101	Western Civilization I **or**
HIS 102	Western Civilization II
GEO 101	World Geography
GOV 102	American Government
SOC 102	General Sociology
CEY 201	Courtship, Marriage and Family
PSY 102	Intro. To Psychology

Humanities   9 credit hrs. /144 clock hrs.

Choose 3 of the following courses (3 hours must be language):

MUS 201	Practical Music Skills
MUS 202	Music Appreciation
DRM 202	Drama
SPA 201	Spanish I
SPA 202	Spanish II

Music Concentration only requires 3 credit hrs./48 clock hrs.

Bachelor of Arts in Bible and Theology (Pre-Seminary) Major

Requirements 84 credit hrs./1344 clock hrs. in addition to 40 credit hours/624 clock hrs. General Ed. Credits (124 credit hrs./2032 clock hrs. total)

BIBLE FUNDAMENTALS   12 credit hours/192 clock hours

BIB 101   Old Testament Survey

BIB 102   New Testament Survey

BIB 203   Hermeneutics

BIB 204   Gospel of John (Inductive Study)

BIBLE   30 credit hours/480 clock hours

Old Testament

OLD 202   Pentateuch

OLD 302   Historical Books

OLD 301   Major Prophets **or**

OLD 303   Minor Prophets

OLD 401   Poetics and Wisdom Literature

OLD 402   Daniel and Revelation

New Testament

NEW 202   Life of Christ

NEW 302   Acts of the Apostles

NEW 401   Romans and Galatians

NEW 303   General Epistles **or**

NEW 313   Prison and Pastoral Epistles

NEW 402   I and II Corinthians

Biblical Languages   12 credit hours/192 clock hours

GRE 301   Elementary Greek I

GRE 302   Elementary Greek II

GRE 401   Intermediate Greek I

GRE 402	Intermediate Greek II

Theology   **18 credit hours/288 clock hours**

THE 201	Christian Theology I
THE 202	Christian Theology II
THE 301	Christian Ethics
THE 302	Pentecostal History and Theology
HIS 302	Church History
THE 401	Apologetics

Practical Ministry   **15 credit hours/256 clock hours**

MIN 301	Homiletics
SFD 208	Spiritual Formation/Discipleship
PRM 432	Senior Seminar
PRM 428	Internship
Chapel	

Bachelor of Science in Christian Ministry Major

Requirements 84 credit hrs./1344 clock hrs. in addition to 40 credit hrs./624 clock hrs. General Ed. Courses (124 credit hrs./2032 clock hrs. total)

Concentration

Pastoral Studies

Church Education/Youth Ministry

Missions

Music

Bible   **30 credit hours/480 clock hrs.**

Old Testament

OLD 302	Historical Books
OLD 301	Major Prophets **or**

OLD 303	Minor Prophets
OLD 401	Poetic and Wisdom Literature
OLD 402	Daniel and Revelation

New Testament

NEW 202	Life of Christ
NEW 302	Acts of the Apostles
NEW 401	Romans and Galatians
NEW 303	General Epistles **or**
NEW 313	Prison and Pastoral Epistles
NEW 402	I and II Corinthians

Foundation Studies   15 credit hrs./240 clock hrs.

BIB 101	Old Testament Survey
BIB 102	New Testament Survey
MIN 201	Life and Work of the Minister
BIB 203	Hermeneutics
BIB 204	Gospel of John (Inductive Study)

Theology   18 credit hrs./288 clock hrs.

THE 201	Christian Theology I
THE 202	Christian Theology II
THE 301	Christian Ethics
THE 302	Pentecostal History and Theology
HIS 302	Church History
THE 401	Apologetics

(Music Concentration requires 15 credit hours/240 clock hours of theology)

PASTORAL STUDIES TRACK

Requirements (Pastoral Studies)   24 credit hrs./432 clock hrs.

| MIS 203 | Church Planting and Revitalization |

MIN 301	Homiletics I
MIN 302	Homiletics II
MIN 401	Pastoral Theology/Church Administration
SFD 208	Spiritual Formation/Discipleship
PRM 432	Senior Seminar
PRM 428	Internship
Chapel	

Electives

CEY 301	Church Education Ministries
CEY 302	Youth and Children's Ministries
HEB 302	Intro. To Biblical Hebrew
MIN 202	Intro. To Counseling
MIS 301	Strategies for Evangelism and Missions
MIS 302	Evangelism and Church Growth

CHRISTIAN EDUCATION/YOUTH MINISTRIES TRACK
Requirements (Christian Education/Youth Ministries)
21 credit hrs./336 clock hrs.

MIN 301	Homiletics I
CEY 301	Church Education Ministries
CEY 302	Youth and Children's Ministries
SFD 208	Spiritual Formation/Discipleship
PRM 432	Senior Seminar
Elective	(From list below)
PRM 428	Internship

Electives

HEB 302	Intro. To Biblical Hebrew
MIN 302	Homiletics II
MIN 401	Pastoral Theology/Church Administration

MIS 203	Church Planting/Revitalization
MIS 301	Strategies for Evangelism and Missions
MIS 302	Evangelism and Church Growth
PSY 201	Developmental Psychology

MISSIONS TRACK

Requirements (Missions) 21 credit hrs./336 clock hrs.

MIN 301	Homiletics I
SFD 208	Spiritual Formation
PRM 432	Senior Seminar
MIS 301	Strategies for Evangelism and Missions **or**
MIS 302	Evangelism and Church Growth
MIS 401	Cross-Cultural Communications
MIS 402	Contemporary World and Missions
PRM 428	Internship

MUSIC TRACK

Requirements (Music)   21 credit hrs./336 clock hrs.

MUS 201	Practical Music Skills
MUS 202	Music History/Appreciation
MUS 203	Applied Piano
MUS 213	Applied Voice
MUS 206	Ensemble
MUS 301	Music Ministry/Leadership
MUS 302	Conducting
MUS 401	Music Theory I
MUS 402	Music Theory II

Practical   **12 credit hours/144 clock hours**

| PRM 428 | Internship |

PRM 432   Senior Seminar

SFD 208   Spiritual Formation

Chapel

BEAM PROGRAM

BEAM students have a separate degree.

A. This would be in the form of a B.Th. The B.Th is a religious studies degree aimed at second vocation students or older students that desire to work in the church only.

   2. B.Th Degree is only for BEAM students.

   3. B.Th classes are for BEAM students only.

   4. B.S. or B.A. students will not be accepted into these classes without the Academic Dean's written approval and a written plan for extra studies by the Professor.

B. This degree would be awarded to the student that completes five of six modules. (3x5=15x6=90 credit hrs.) The module can be obtained as a standalone study or as a group for the B.Th degree.

C. Each module will be comprised of six 3 hr. classes. The module can be accomplished in one semester.

D. Two module programs will be offered each semester.

   1. The degree cycle will be three years

E. The classes will be given in one of the following formats:

   1. DVD/Thumb drive/…

   2. In-house class for more than three students

   3. ZOOM for classes of 3 or less

   4. YouTube Channel (school will set up channel for class needs)

   5. Directed studies only for students with the Academic Dean's approval

F. Module Programs

   1. Pastoral Ministries

   2. Pastoral Care and Counseling

3. Christian Education: Spiritual Formation and Discipleship
4. Church Growth and Planting
5. Biblical Studies I
6. Biblical Studies II

Three Year Class Schedule for BEAM Classes

BTh (Bachelor of Practical Theology Degree)
108 credit hrs./810 clock hrs.
1st Semester
Bible I: 18 credit hrs./135 clock hrs.
Tuesday
Session 1
1. Spiritual Formation
2. Religious History
Session 2
3. Study of the Gospels
4. Introduction to the O.T.
Session 3
5. Apologetics
6. New Testament Theology

2nd Semester
Christian Education   18 credit hrs./135 clock hrs.
Tuesday
Session 1
1. Introduction to Christian Education
2. Religious Writing
Session 2
3. Discipleship

4. Christian Formation of Children

Session 3

5. How to Teach for Learning

6. Christian Formation for Adults

3rd Semester

Bible II   **18 credit hrs./135 clock hrs.**

Tuesday

Session 1

1. Spiritual Formation

2. Pentecostal History

Session 2

3. Pauline Studies

4. Introduction to the New Testament

Session 3

5. The General Epistles

6. Apocalyptic Studies

4th Semester

Pastoral Care/Counseling   **18 credit hrs./135 clock hrs.**

Thursday

Session 1

1. Spiritual Formation

2. Religious Writing

Session 2

3. Community Chaplaincy

4. Pastoral Counseling

Session 3

5. The Ministry Role in Healing

6. Family Ministries

5th Semester

Church Growth   **18 credit hrs./135 clock hrs.**

Thursday

Session 1

1. Spiritual Formation

2. Bible History

Session 2

3. Church Planting Essentials

4. Church Revitalization

Session 3

5. Churches Planting Churches

6. Cross Cultural Ministries

6th Semester

Pastoral Ministries   **18 credit hrs./135 clock hrs.**

Thursday

Session 1

1. Spiritual Formation

2. Religious Writing

Session 2

3. Church Administration

4. Leadership in the Modern Churches

Session 3

5. Contemporary Issues in Secular and Church Culture

6. Creative Ministries

TOTAL 108 credit hrs./810 clock hrs.

(Degree requirement totals: 90 credit hrs./675 clock hrs.)

Bachelor of Arts in Bible and Theology (Pre-Seminary)
Recommended Course of Study

FRESHMAN YEAR
Fall Semester

ENG 101 English Composition I	3
Freshman Orientation	1
BIB 101 Old Testament Survey	3
HIS 101 Western Civilization I **or** II	3
GEO 101 World Geography **or**	
GOV 102 American Government	3
SFD 208 Spiritual Formation	1
Chapel	.5
Total	14.5 hours

Spring Semester

ENG 102 English Composition II	3
FIN 102 Personal Money Management	3
BIB 102 New Testament Survey	3
PSY 102 Intro. To Psychology	3
SOC 102 General Sociology	3
SFD 208 Spiritual Formation	1
Chapel	.5
Total	16.5 hours

SOPHOMORE YEAR
Fall Semester

CEY 201 Courtship, Marriage	3

Humanities (elective)	3
THE 201 Christian Theology I	3
BIB 203 Hermeneutics	3
SFD 208 Spiritual Formation	1
Chapel	.5
Total	13.5 hours

Spring Semester

BIB 204 Gospel of John	3
NEW 202 Life of Christ	3
OLD 202 Pentateuch	3
Humanities (Elective)	3
SFD 208 Spiritual Formation	1
THE 202 Christian Theology II	3
Chapel	.5
Total	16.5 hours

JUNIOR YEAR

Fall Semester

OLD 301 Major Prophets **or**	
OLD 303 Minor Prophets	3
Humanities (elective)	3
MIN 301 Homiletics I	3
GRE 301 Elementary Greek I	3
THE 301 Christian Ethics	3
Chapel	.5
Total	15.5 hours

Spring Semester

GRE 302 Elementary Greek II	3
NEW 302 Acts of the Apostles	3
HIS 302 Church History	3
THE 302 Pent. Hist. & Theology	3
OLD 302 Historical Books	3
Chapel	.5
Total	15.5 hours

Summer

PRM 428 Internship	3

SENIOR YEAR

Fall Semester

NEW 401 Romans and Galatians	3
OLD 401 Poetic & Wisdom Lit.	3
GRE 401 Intermediate Greek I	3
THE 401 Apologetics	3
PRM 432 Senior Seminar	2
New Testament Elective	3
Total	17 hours

Spring Semester

New Testament Elective	3
ENG 402 Survey of Literature	3
GRE 402 Intermediate Greek II	3
OLD 402 Daniel and Revelation	3
Total	12 hours

TOTAL HOURS   **124 credit hrs./2160 Clock hrs.**

Bachelor of Science in Christian Ministry
Pastoral Studies Track
Recommended Course of Study

FRESHMAN YEAR
Fall Semester

ENG 101 English Composition I	3
Freshman Orientation	1
BIB 101 Old Testament Survey	3
HIS 101 Western Civ. I **or** II	3
GEO 101 World Geography **or**	
GOV 102 American Government	3
SFD 208 Spiritual Formation	1
Chapel	.5
Total	14.5 hours

Spring Semester

ENG 102 English Composition II	3
FIN 102 Personal Money Management	3
BIB 102 New Testament Survey	3
PSY 102 Intro. To Psychology	3
SOC 102 General Sociology	3
SFD 208 Spiritual Formation	1
Chapel	.5
Total	16.5 hours

SOPHOMORE YEAR

Fall Semester

CEY 201 Courtship, Marriage	3
MIN 201 Life & Work of the Minister	3
Humanities (elective)	3
THE 201 Christian Theology I	3
BIB 203 Hermeneutics	3
SFD 208 Spiritual Formation	1
Chapel	.5
Total	16.5 hours

Spring Semester

BIB 204 Gospel of John	3
NEW 202 Life of Christ	3
OLD 202 Pentateuch	3
Humanities (elective)	3
THE 202 Christian Theology II	3
SFD 208 Spiritual Formation	1
Chapel	.5
Total	16.5 hours

JUNIOR YEAR

Fall Semester

OLD 301 Major Prophets **or**	
OLD 303 Minor Prophets	3
Humanities (elective)	3
MIN 301 Homiletics	3
THE 301 Christian Ethics	3
Chapel	.5
Total	12.5 hours

Spring Semester

MIN 302 Homiletics II	3
NEW 302 Acts of the Apostles	3
HIS 302 Church History	3
THE 302 Pent. Hist. & Theology	3
OLD 302 Historical Books	3
Chapel	.5
Total	15.5 hours

Summer

PRM 428 Internship	3

SENIOR YEAR

Fall Semester

NEW 401 Romans and Galatians	3
OLD 401 Poetic and Wisdom Lit.	3
MIN 401 Past. Theo. & Church Admin.	3
THE 401 Apologetics	3
PRM 432 Senior Seminar	2
New Testament Elective	3
Total	17 hours

Spring Semester

New Testament Elective	3
ENG 402 Survey of Literature	3
Mis 203 Church Planting/Revitalization	3
OLD 402 Daniel and Revelation	3
Total	12 hours

Total hours: **124 Credit hrs./2160 Clock hrs.**

Bachelor of Science in Christian Ministry
Christian Education/Youth Ministries Track
Recommended Course of Study

FRESHMAN YEAR
Fall Semester

ENG 101 English Composition I	3
Freshman Orientation	1
BIB 101 Old Testament Survey	3
HIS 101 Western Civilization I **or**	
HIS 102 Western Civilization II	3
GEO 101 World Geography **or**	
GOV 102 American Government	3
SFD 208 Spiritual Formation	1
Chapel	.5
Total	14.5 hours

Spring Semester

ENG 102 English Composition II	3
FIN 102 Personal Money Management	3
BIB 102 New Testament Survey	3
PSY 102 Intro. To Psychology	3
SOC 102 General Sociology	3
SFD 208 Spiritual Formation	1
Chapel	.5
Total	16.5 hours

SOPHOMORE YEAR

Fall Semester

CEY 201 Courtship, Marriage	3
MIN 201 Life & work of the Minister	3
Humanities (Elective)	3
THE 201 Christian Theology I	3
BIB 203 Hermeneutics	3
SFD 208 Spiritual Formation	1
Chapel	.5
Total	16.5 hours

Spring Semester

BIB 204 Gospel of John	3
NEW 202 Life of Christ	3
OLD 202 Pentateuch	3
Humanities (elective)	3
THE 202 Christian Theology II	3
SFD 208 Spiritual Formation	1
Chapel	.5
Total	6.5 hours

JUNIOR YEAR

Fall Semester

OLD 301 Major Prophets **or**	
OLD 303 Minor Prophets	3
Humanities (elective)	3
MIN 301 Homiletics I	3
CEY 301 Church Education Ministries	3
THE 301 Christian Ethics	3
Chapel	.5
Total	15.5 hours

Spring Semester

CEY 302 Youth and Children's Ministries	3
NEW 302 Acts of the Apostles	3
HIS 302 Church History	3
THE 302 Pentecostal History & Theology	3
OLD 302 Historical Books	3
Chapel	.5
Total	15.5 hours

SUMMER

PRM 428 Internship	3

SENIOR YEAR

Fall Semester

NEW 401 Romans and Galatians	3
OLD 401 Poetic and Wisdom Literature	3
THE 401 Apologetics	3
New Testament Elective	3
PRM 432 Senior Seminar	2
Total	14 hours

Spring Semester

New Testament Elective	3
ENG 402 Survey of Literature	3
Elective	3
OLD 402 Daniel and Revelation	3
Total	12 hours

Total hours   **124 credit hrs./2160 clock hrs.**

Bachelor of Science in Christian Ministry
Missions Track
Recommended Course of Study

FRESHMAN YEAR
Fall Semester

ENG 101 English Composition I	3
Freshman Orientation	1
BIB 101 Old Testament Survey	3
HIS 101 Western Civ. I **or** II	3
GEO 101 World Geography **or**	
GOV 102 American Government	3
SFD 208 Spiritual Formation	1
Chapel	.5
Total	14.5 hours

Spring Semester

ENG 102 English Composition II	3
FIN 102 Personal Money Management	3
BIB 102 New Testament Survey	3
PSY 102 Intro. To Psychology	3
SOC 102 General Sociology	3
SFD 208 Spiritual Formation	1
Chapel	.5
Total	16.5 hours

SOPHOMORE YEAR
Fall Semester

CEY 201 Courtship, Marriage	3

MIN 201 Life & Work of the Minister	3
THE 201 Christian Theology I	3
Humanities (elective)	3
BIB 203 Hermeneutics	3
SFD 208 Spiritual Formation	1
Chapel	.5
Total	16.5 hours

Spring Semester

BIB 204 Gospel of John	3
NEW 202 Life of Christ	3
SFD 208 Spiritual Formation	1
Humanities (Elective)	3
THE 202 Christian Theology II	3
OLD 202 Pentateuch	3
Chapel	.5
Total	16.5

JUNIOR YEAR

Fall Semester

OLD 301 Major Prophets **or**	
OLD 303 Minor Prophets	3
MIS 301 Strategies for Evangelism & Missions **or**	
MIS 302 Evangelism & Church Growth	3
Humanities (elective)	3
MIN 301 Homiletics I	3
THE 301 Christian Ethics	3
Chapel	.5
Total	15.5 hours

Spring Semester

MIS 302 Evangelism & Church Growth **or**	
MIS 301 Strategies for Evangelism & Missions	3
NEW 302 Acts of the Apostles	3
HIS 302 Church History	3
THE 302 Pentecostal History & Theology	3
OLD 302 Historical Books	3
Chapel	.5
Total	15.5 hours

SUMMER

PRM 428 Internship	3

SENIOR YEAR

Fall Semester

NEW 401 Romans and Galatians	3
OLD 401 Poetic & Wisdom Literature	3
MIS 401 Cross-Cultural Communications	3
THE 401 Apologetics	3
New Testament Elective	3
PRM 432 Senior Seminar	2
Total	17 hours

Spring Semester

New Testament Elective	3
ENG 402 Survey of Literature	3
MIS 402 Contemporary World & Missions	3
OLD 402 Daniel and Revelation	3
Total	12 hours
Total hours	**124 credit hrs./2160 clock hrs.**

Bachelor of Science in Christian Ministry
Music Track
Recommended Course of Study

FRESHMAN YEAR
Fall Semester

ENG 101 English Composition I	3
Freshman Orientation	1
BIB 101 Old Testament Survey	3
HIS 101 Western Civilization I **or**	
HIS 102 Western Civilization II	3
GEO 101 World Geography **or**	
GOV 102 American Government	3
SFD 208 Spiritual Formation	1
Chapel	.5
Total	14.5 hours

Spring Semester

ENG 102 English Composition II	3
FIN 102 Personal Money Management	3
BIB 102 New Testament Survey	3
PSY 102 Intro. To Psychology	3
SOC 102 General Sociology	3
SFD 208 Spiritual Formation	1
Chapel	.5
Total	16.5 hours

SOPHOMORE YEAR
Fall Semester

CEY 201 Courtship, Marriage	3
MIN 201 Life & Work of the Minister	3
MUS 201 Practical Music Skills	3
THE 201 Christian Theology I	3
BIB 203 Hermeneutics	3
SFD 208 Spiritual Formation	1
Chapel	.5
Total	16.5 hours

Spring Semester

BIB 204 Gospel of John	3
NEW 202 Life of Christ	3
OLD 202 Pentateuch	3
MUS 202 Music History/Appreciation	2
THE 202 Christian Theology II	3
SFD 208 Spiritual Formation	1
Chapel	.5
Total	15.5 hours

JUNIOR YEAR
Fall Semester

OLD 301 Major Prophets **or**	
OLD 303 Minor Prophets	3
Humanities (elective)	3
MIN 301 Homiletics I	3
MUS 301 Music Min./Leadership	3
THE 301 Christian Ethics	3

MUS 206 Ensemble	1
MUS 203 Applied Piano I	1
Chapel	.5
Total	17.5 hours

Spring Semester

MUS 302 Conducting	1
NEW 302 Acts of the Apostles	3
HIS 302 Church History	3
THE 302 Pentecostal History & Theology	3
OLD 302 Historical Books	3
MUS 203 Applied Piano II	1
Chapel	.5
Total	14.5 hours

SUMMER

PRM 428 Internship	3

SENIOR YEAR

Fall Semester

MUS 401 Music Theory I	3
NEW 401 Romans and Galatians	3
OLD 401 Poetic and Wisdom Literature	3
THE 401 Apologetics	3
New Testament Elective	3
PRM 432 Senior Seminar	2
MUS 213 Applied Voice I	1
Total	18 hours

Spring Semester

MUS 402 Music Theory II	3
New Testament Elective	3
ENG 402 Survey of Literature	3
OLD 402 Daniel and Revelation	3
MIS 213 Applied Voice II	1
MUS 206 Ensemble	1
Total	13 hours

Total Hours: **124 credit hrs./2160 clock hrs.**

Course Descriptions

BIBLE

BIB 101 Old Testament Survey   3 credits

A broad study of the Old Testament within historical and cultural contexts. The course broadly examines the writer, message, date, and audience of each Old Testament book.

BIB 102 New Testament Survey   3 credits

A broad study of the New Testament within historical and cultural contexts. The course broadly examines the writer, message, date, and audience of each New Testament book.

BIB 203 Hermeneutics   3 credits

An introduction to the principles and processes of interpreting the Bible, with an emphasis on the grammatical-historical method. Students will learn to utilize resources and make practical application from the biblical text.

BIB 204 Gospel of John (Inductive)   3 credits

This study emphasizes the inductive process of observation-investigation, interpretation, and assimilation. A passage is studied in light of book, chapter, and paragraph with emphasis on context.

OLD 202 Pentateuch   3 credits

An expository and theological study of the Old Testament books known by the Greek name Pentateuch: Genesis, Exodus, Leviticus, Numbers, and Deuteronomy. The course will explore a pattern for a God-centered worldview in five complimentary portraits of the person of God: His sovereignty over His creation, His covenantal faithfulness in redeeming man for service, His desire for fellowship with man through holiness, His wise and caring leadership of His people, and His unique position as the only proper object of man's devotion.

NEW 202 Life of Christ   3 credits

A study of the life of Jesus Christ. The course will focus on the major events surrounding Christ's life on earth within the context of first century Jewish culture. Included in this study will be the context and message of Jesus' parables as well as examination of the supernatural expressions of Christ's power through miracles.

OLD 301 Major Prophets   **3 credits**

An expository and theological study of the Old Testament prophetic books, Isaiah, Jeremiah, Lamentations of Jeremiah, Ezekiel, and Daniel. Each book is examined with respect to historical background, major literary and textual critical questions, a biographical sketch of the prophet, and theological emphasis.

OLD 302 Historical Books   **3 credits**

This course will examine the period of the Old Testament from Joshua and the conquest of Canaan to the Babylonian Captivity. In addition, Ezra, Nehemiah, and Esther will be considered. The course will develop an appreciation of notable persons and events of this period. Special emphasis will be given to the Abrahamic and Davidic covenants as they unfold in the historical books.

NEW 302 Acts of the Apostles   **3 credits**

A study of the Book of Acts. This course examines the lives and ministries of the original apostles as presented in the New Testament.

OLD 303 Minor Prophets   **3 credits**

This course examines the history, text, milieu, structure, and theological purpose of each of the minor prophets. Special emphasis will be given the prophetic themes of each book, such as: the "call to repentance", the "judgments of the various nations", and the coming "Day of the Lord."

NEW 303 General Epistles   **3 credits**

A systematic study of James, the Petrine Epistles, Hebrews, Jude, and the Johannine Epistles. The course examines the theology and doctrine of these books within the larger framework of New Testament studies.

NEW 313 Prison and Pastoral Epistles   **3 credits**

A systematic study of Ephesians, Colossians, Philippians, Philemon, I and II Timothy, and Titus. The course examines the life of Paul as well as Pauline doctrine.

OLD 401 Poetic and Wisdom Literature   **3 credits**

A study of Psalms, Proverbs, Ecclesiastes, and the Song of Solomon. The course focuses on the relevance of these books to the Postmodern world.

NEW 401 Romans and Galatians   3 credits

A systematic study of Romans and Galatians. The course emphasizes the cardinal Christian doctrines found in these books.

OLD 402 Daniel and Revelation   3 credits

An eschatological study of Daniel and Revelation. The course focuses on the different interpretations of end-time literature and seeks to develop a proper understanding of futuristic events.

NEW 402 I and II Corinthians   3 credits

A systematic study of I and II Corinthians. The course examines the theology of these books in light of the cultural and historical setting of Corinth.

GENERAL EDUCATION COURSES

English and Communication

ENG 101 English Composition I   3 credits

An introduction to written English. The course examines grammar and composition and requires a research paper.

ENG 102 English Composition II   3 credits

A study of expression and writing skills at the level of the word, sentence, paragraph, and complete essay. A full-length research paper is required.

ESL/ELL: English as a Second Language/English Language Learner

Prerequisite before enrolling in English 101 for all non-native English speakers   3 credits

The main purpose of an ESL instructor is to help provide non-native English speakers the opportunity to acquire fluency in the English language, both in the written and spoken word. However, the core reading subskill is forming connections between speech and print. Subsequently, phonological awareness is foundational for a true grasp of decoding skills in learning any language that employs an alphabetic system. Spoken words are sequences of phonemes and are represented by letters in the English language, which is the fundamental literary principle that must be thoroughly mastered. Thus, the ESL class will start at this foundational level. After which, students will learn how to apply various spelling and grammar principles to enhance their reading and writing skills. Mastery to automaticity is the goal.

ENG 402 Survey of Literature   **3 credits**

An introduction to literary terms and forms. The course examines a broad selection of famous literary works.

Math and Science

Freshman Orientation   **1 credit**

A course designed to orient the student to college life at Holmes Bible College. Special attention will be given to study habits, rules and policies, historical setting, and adaptation to the college environment.

FIN 102 Personal Money Management   **3 credits**

A comprehensive study of the various aspects of finance that relate to the individual and/or family.

Social Sciences

HIS 101 Western Civilization I   **3 credits**

A study of the history of man from his beginning to the Renaissance. The course focuses on the history of man in the Western world.

HIS 102 Western Civilization II   **3 credits**

A study of Western history from the Renaissance to the present. The course amplifies the role of the church in history.

GOV 101 World Geography   **3 credits**

An introduction to world geography. The course examines location, anthropology, languages, people groups, and social units with a special emphasis on the geography of Bible lands.

GOV 102 American Government   **3 credits**

An introduction to the processes and policies of American government. The course focuses on the Constitution, the development of public policy, and modern political events.

SOC 102 General Sociology   **3 credits**

Introduction to the principal concepts, methods, and terminology of sociology. The relation of culture to group activities and an analysis of the major social institutions.

PSY 102 Introduction to Psychology   3 credits

Introduction to the science of psychology through investigations of the fundamental conditions and facts of thought and behavior, including the physiological basis of behavior, personality, emotions, feelings, sensations, learning, habit formation, memory, and perception.

PSY 201 Developmental Psychology or Life Span Development

Prerequisite: Introduction to Psychology

The Developmental Psychology or Life Span Psychology course is designed to introduce students to the systematic and scientific study of the behavior and mental processes of human beings. The course focuses on human growth and development throughout the life cycle and examines normal developmental stages with an emphasis on the physical, spiritual, intellectual, social, and emotive progressions. However, psychology as an academic discipline at Holmes Bible College will be carefully evaluated in light of biblical principles and will not be reticent to address issues where Scripture and psychology seem to be in tension.

CEY 201 Courtship, Marriage and Family   3 credits

An examination of Biblical principles of romantic and family relationships. The course focuses on temperament studies, gender roles, and child rearing.

Humanities

MUS 201 Practical Music Skills   3 credits

An introductory course to music designed for the student to gain music skills to sing, lead and read music. This course will equip the student with the knowledge to address the music program in a church they may pastor.

MUS 202 Music Appreciation   3 credits

A survey of musical styles and historical pieces. The course includes an introduction to famous historical and modern musical pieces.

DRM/SPH 201/202 Drama/Speech   3 credits

Speech and Drama courses 201 (Fall) and 202 (Spring) are designed to develop the following long-term goals: communication skills, acting skills, listening skills, language skills, self-discipline, teamwork, and leadership. These elements are conveyed through subjects as diverse as storytelling, interpretation of poetry, readers theater, debating, and acting. Theory and technique combine to instruct the student in presenting characterizations, narratives, poetry, stories, monologues, acting scenes, readers theater, radio broadcasts, biographies, improvisations, theater history, sermons and more. The student will find many academic advantages resulting from this study that extend beyond the discipline of drama. The speech component of the course is designed to give students the best possible training in public speaking and communication. Performing various types of literature improves comprehension of and appreciation for literature. Learning to communicate publicly can develop confidence balanced with dependence on the Lord; therefore, the course is purposefully designed to refine the communication skills of the Christian student for the Lord's service. "Not by might, not by power, but by My Spirit says the Lord" (Zechariah. 4:6).

SPA 201 Spanish I   3 credits

The fundamentals of Spanish grammar. The course introduces the student to the rudiments of modern Spanish.

SPA 202 Spanish II   3 credits

The fundamentals of Spanish grammar continued. This course continues the study begun in SPA 201.

Biblical Languages

GRE 301 Elementary Greek I   3 credits

An introduction to New Testament Koine Greek. The course focuses on grammar, vocabulary, transition, and pronunciation of the New Testament text.

GRE 302 Elementary Greek II   3 credits

An introduction to exegesis. The course includes word studies.

GRE 401 Intermediate Greek I   3 credits

Further development of the Greek vocabulary and grammatical rules of exegesis. The course provides a more detailed study of Grammar.

GRE 402 Intermediate Greek II   3 credits

An application of the grammatical and exegetical principles of Greek. The course provides theoretical knowledge of New Testament Greek in a practical way to pursue Greek studies beyond the classroom.

HEB 301 Intro. To Biblical Hebrew   **3 credits**

This course is a study of the fundamentals of Biblical Hebrew grammar, syntax, and vocabulary. It is the foundation for interpretation of the Hebrew Old Testament.

Theology

THE 201 Christian Theology I   **3 credits**

An introduction to the task, resources, and method of doing theology. Included are the doctrines of the Scriptures, God, Man, and Jesus Christ. The course examines the historical context, the biblical basis and the application for life and ministry of each doctrine.

THE 202 Christian Theology II   **3 credits**

An introduction to the doctrines of the Holy Spirit, the application of redemption, the Church, and eschatology. The course examines the historical context, the biblical basis, and the application for life and ministry of each doctrine.

THE 301 Christian Ethics   **3 credits**

An introduction to the methodology and content of biblical Christian ethics with application to the specific contemporary issues of human rights, politics, economics, war, and peace, racism, sexuality, and biomedical concerns. The course focuses on a Christ-centered approach to character development and moral decision-making.

THE 302 Pentecostal History and Theology 3 credits

A study of the history, development, and theology of the Holiness/Pentecostal movement. The course focuses on modern Pentecostalism including a study of the Great Azusa Street Revival in 1906.

HIS 302 Church History   **3 credits**

An introduction to the history of Christianity from apostolic to modern times. The course will examine turning points of the Church age such as the councils, the rise and fall of various doctrines, church and state relationships, Protestantism, the rise of denominations, and encounter with both modernism and postmodernism.

THE 401 Apologetics   **3 credits**

Introduction to Apologetics serves to prepare the student with the ability to correctly interpret and successfully convey the Word of God in an assortment of contexts and to give a rational explanation of the doctrines that are essential to Scripture and to champion the historic Christian faith.

Practical Ministry

MIN 201 Life and Work of the Minister   **3 credits**

An introduction to the basic concepts, theologies, and practices of practical Christian ministry. The course serves as a general approach to the entire major.

MIN 202 Pastoral/Biblical Counseling   **3 credits**

The Pastoral/Biblical Counseling course prepares students for a ministry of counseling in local churches, in local/foreign missions, in summer camps, in biblical counseling centers, and in other settings in which people seek help for life's challenges. Biblical Counseling provides training for clergy, lay pastoral counselors, and Christian school teachers. The class will build on a core biblical knowledge base while learning advanced mental health counseling skills. Students also receive training that draws from a variety of clinical and pastoral fields presented from a Christian perspective that values the unique God-given identity of every individual. Knowledge of the Scriptures and an understanding of human personality are combined in teaching pastoral/biblical counseling. Though psychology and theology are integrated to some extent, the class will retain a priority on evangelical doctrine and biblical authority.

MIN 301 Homiletics I   **3 credits**

A study of the elements of preaching. The course focuses on the practical elements of preparing and delivering a sermon.

MIN 302 Homiletics II   **3 credits**

A study of the elements of storytelling in sermons. The course includes practical preparation for preaching including narration and stories within sermons.

MIN 401 Pastoral Theology and Church Admin.   **3 credits**

To study and understand the theory and practice of pastoral work.

MIS 203 Church Planting and Revitalization   3 credits

An introduction to the modern movement of the Holy Spirit in the Pentecostal and Evangelical communities to plant new churches in the United States and abroad. This class will focus on the Biblical basis for church planting and on the practical values and know-how that lead to successful church plants.

PRM 428 Internship   3 credits

The internship must consist of at least 200 hours of supervised, approved ministry experience. Internship requirements are handled through the Academic Affairs Office.

PRM 432 Senior Seminar/Thesis   2 credits

A concluding seminar and reflection thesis that culminates the educational experience and launches the student into ministry.

SFD 208 Spiritual Formation   1-4 credits

The practice of community, growth, and maturity. The course consists of a journey toward God.

SFD 208 Spiritual Formation and SFD 428 Internship
BEAM Requirement   6 credits

These courses are combined to meet the requirements of the BEAM students who are assigned five weeks of intensive field experience along with the Spiritual Formation course concurrently. Students work with the instructor to journal and respond to oversight of the field experience personnel as well as to complete readings as assigned. The Spiritual Formation segment will be taught in five week segments and require readings and written projects.

PRM 432 Senior Seminar   2 credits

Senior Seminar is required by seniors and is offered concurrently with the above courses. The senior seminar requires a thesis and assigned readings to conclude the BEAM schedule. (This is specifically for seniors graduating at the end of the current semester).

Concentration Courses

CEY 301 Church Education Ministries   3 credits

An overview study of the various representative Christian Education ministries within the local church. This course gives students a foundational understanding of the structure and functions of the local church. Special attention is given to the personal, interpersonal, family, and professional dimensions of ministry. Attention is also given to the role of the church in making disciples in response to the Great Commission.

CEY 302 Youth and Children's Ministries   3 credits

A survey of the various stages of child and adolescent development and ministry techniques for each. The course examine discipline teaching methods, and a salvation presentation in light of changing cultural mores.

MUS 301 Music Ministry/Leadership   3 credits

This course is designed to introduce students to elements of a music **leader** and their relationship with the church body. Students will study a biblical foundation to worship and its important role in ministry of a music leader. There will be a study on contemporary music, various artists, and their impact on today's music ministry.

MUS 302 Basic Conducting   1 credit

Includes practical experience in basic conducting patterns, cuing of entrances and exits, tempo, dynamic and score reading of basic choral repertoire.

Chapel   3 credits

Chapel is inspirational worship, proclamation of the Word, education, celebration, and informational dissemination. A wide variety of speakers and worship experiences are offered.

MUS 203-206 Applied Piano   1 credit

Basic keyboard skills are developed through a study of scales, chords, and cadences. Repertoire will be selected according to the student's level.

MIS 301 Strategies for Evangelism and Missions   3 credits

A study of problems and principles involved in the development of strategy of the communication of the Gospel in the various cultures of the world. Case studies are used to demonstrate the application of principles.

MIS 302 Evangelism and Church Growth   3 credits

A study of problems and principles involved in the development of strategy for the communication of the gospel and church growth.

MIS 401 Cross-Cultural Communications   3 credits

Addressed the theory and challenges of communications in general and the unique challenges of effective cross-cultural communication in particular.

MIS 402 The Contemporary World and Missions   3 credits

A critical evaluation of the concepts and programs of significant movements effecting contemporary missions. Emphasis is placed on partnership, ecumenism, liberation theology, contextualization, urbanization, church growth, spiritual warfare and the second coming of Christ. Careful consideration is given to the responsibility of the church and the missionary in the light of these trends.

MUS 213-216 Applied Voice   1 credit

Students will be introduced to physical exercises to improve their vocal range, ear training, breath control, tone production and enunciation. Repertoire will be selected according to the student's level.

MUS 207 Ensemble   1 credit

The ensemble will be open to the entire student body. As in voice, students will be introduced to physical exercise to improve their vocal range, ear training, breath control, tone production and enunciation as well as blend. Repertoire will be selected according to the ensembles level.

MUS 401 Music Theory I   3 credits

The fundamentals of music (Mus 201 Practical Music Skills) will be reviewed. Additional studies in elementary part-writing, cadences, and inversions and simple melodic compositions will be introduced.

MUS 402 Music Theory II   3 credits

Continued development of skills begun in MUS 401 and study of secondary triads, dominant 7th chords, and common harmonic progressions.

Holmes Bible College

Campus Buildings

The land was purchased and dedicated on October 16, 1998. It is 39.6 acres. Purchase price - $1,276,754.50

Paul Franklin Beacham Learning Center - dedicated in October 2008. Named for Dr. Paul F. Beacham, who served as president for 59 years (1919-1978). $1, 900,000.00

Brooks-King Missions Duplex – dedicated on September 30, 2010, in memory of Rev. and Mrs. John W. Brooks and Rev. and Mrs. Henry King. $186,717.18

Tripp-Van Dyke Residence Hall for Men – dedicated on February 24, 2012, and named in memory/honor of the Tripp and Van Dyke families. $565,610.01

President's Home - purchased in 2014 and remodeled by Carl Sturkie. $142,104.11

Holmes Memorial Tabernacle Pentecostal Church - dedicated on August 30, 2015. The former church on the corner of Buncombe and Briggs was organized in 1910 and became known as the Tabernacle Pentecostal Church. In 1919 at the time of Rev. Holmes' death, the church became known as Holmes Memorial Tabernacle Pentecostal Church. $1,091,784.35

Ellenberg Student Center – dedicated on October 5, 2017, and named in honor of the Ellenberg family and those family members who attended the college – Grace, Vernon, Vinson, and Bill. $1,156,220.14

Freeman-Duncan Dormitory for Women – dedicated on March 9, 2018, and named in memory of Rev. and Mrs. D.D. Freeman and Rev. and Mrs. L.M. Duncan. $435,403.38

Leggett Way – dedicated on October 4, 2018, in memory/honor of Bishop James and Mrs. Faye Leggett. $4,000.00

Carl O. Sturkie Maintenance Facility - dedicated on October 17, 2019, in honor of missionaries Rev. and Mrs. Carl Sturkie. $114,878.81

Flag Pole/Brick Yard Project dedicated February 26, 2021: Col. Jack Kelley – Flag Poles, George and Jackie Wilson – Brick Yard. $26,702.70

Prayer and Missions Garden - dedicated February 26, 2021, to Mr. and Mrs. Richard D. Waters. $53,426.52,

Grand Total $6,953,601.70

**Special Note-All of these figures do not include all of the donated hours of labor, which were considerable.

Bibliography

Holiness and Pentecostals Periodicals

The Altamont Witness (Greenville, SC) 1911-1916.

The Pentecostal Holiness Advocate (Royston & Franklin Springs) 1917-1978.

The Christian and Missionary Alliance (Nyack, NY) 1897-1900).

Magazines

The Holmes Bulletin (Greenville, SC) 1942.

The Voice of Holmes (Greenville, SC) 1947-1969.

Holmes Magazine (Greenville, SC) 1998-2004.

A View of Holmes Bible College (Greenville, SC) 2010.

Internet Sources

https://www.presbyteriansofthepast.com/2019/11/11/zelotes-l-holmes/,

Newspapers & Newsletters

Anderson Intelligencer (Anderson, SC) 1899.

The Burlingame Enterprise (Burlingame, KS) 1897.

The Daily Record (Columbia, SC) 1907-1914.

The Laurens Advertiser (Laurens, SC) 1900-1904.

The Louisville Courier-Journal (Louisville, KY) 1897

Hugh's News & Commentary (Watkinsville, GA) 2008, 2017.

Archives

Holmes Bible College Archives. Wills of N. J. Holmes & Lucy. S. Holmes, article by Mrs. Nina Holmes.

David M. Rubenstein Rare Book & Manuscript Library, Duke University. Boxes 1 and 2, N. J. Holmes.

Books

Beacham, A. D. Jr. *Azusa East: The Life and Times of G. B. Cashwell.* Franklin Springs, GA: LifeSprings Resources Publications, 2006.

Benson, John T. Jr. *Holiness Organized or Un Organized? A History 1989-1915 Pentecostal Mission.* Nashville, TN: Trevecca Press, 1977.

Boles, John B. *The Great Revival: Beginnings of the Bible Belt.* Lexington, KY: The University Press of Kentucky, 1996.

Burgess, Stanley M., et al. *Dictionary of Pentecostal/Charismatic Movements.* Grand Rapids, MI: Zondervan, 2002.

Holmes, N. J. and Wife, (Lucy Simpson Holmes). *Life Sketches and Sermons.* Franklin Springs, GA: Publishing House of the Pentecostal Holiness Church, 1920.

Nienkirchen, Charles W. *A. B. Simpson and The Pentecostal Movement: A Study in Continuity, Crisis, and Change.* Eugene, OR: Wipf and Stock Publishers, 1991.

Rack, Henry D. *Reasonable Enthusiast: John Wesley and the Rise of Methodism.* Philadelphia, PA: Trinity Press International, 1989.

Synan, Vinson and Daniel Woods. *Fire Baptized: The Many Lives and Works of Benjamin Hardin Irwin.* Lexington, KY: Emeth Press, 2017.

.....Synan, Vinson. *The Century of the Holy Spirit: 100 Years of Pentecostal and Charismatic Renewal.* Nashville, TN: Thomas Nelson Publishers, 2001.

Thomas, Miss Iva. Private Publication, n.d.

Thornton, Michael. *Fire in the Carolinas: The Revival Legacy of G. B. Cashwell and A. B. Crumpler.* Lake Mary, FL.: Creation House, 2014.

York, H. Stanley. *George Floyd Taylor: The Life of An Early Southern Pentecostal Leader.* Xulon Press: USA, 2013.

Yount, Michael G. *A. B. Simpson: His Message and Impact on the Third Great Awakening.* Eugene, OR: Wipf and Stock Publishers, 2016.

Endnotes

1   https://www.presbyteriansofthepast.com/2019/11/11/zelotes-l-holmes/, Rev. N. J. Holmes and Wife, *Life Sketches and Sermons*, Advocate Press, 1920, 7-8. This source will be referred to as LSS for the remainder of this book.

2   N. J. Holmes will be referred to as Nick for the paper for his younger years. This was the name used for him by others.

3   Ibid. pp. 12-13.

4   Ibid. pp. 13-16.

5   Ibid. pp. 18

6   Ibid. pp. 17-18.

7   Ibid. pp. 20-21.

8   Ibid. pp. 21-23.

9   Ibid. pp. 23.

10   Ibid. p. 27.

11   Ibid. pp. 28.

12   Ibid. pp. 32-35.

13   David M.Rubenstein Rare Book & Manuscript Library, Duke University. This library contains the Holmes Family Collection. Nick Holmes Collection has two boxes. In box two Correspondence 1892-1897 one can find copies of his examination papers from Edinburgh and his first sermon at Clinton, SC. There is no mention of the degree bestowed upon Holmes at Edinburgh, nor does the Holmes Bible College have a record of any degree bestowed upon him.

14   LSS. pp. 57-58.

15   Ibid. pp. 56-57.

16   Ibid. pp. 58-59.

17   Ibid. pp.62-63.

18   Ibid. p. 62.

19   Ibid. pp. 62-63.

20   Ibid. p. 63.

21   Ibid. p. 64.

22   Ibid. pp. 64-65.

23   LSS. p. 68.

24   Ibid. p. 68.

25   For further examination of Sanctification a list of the following books maybe read. *A Plain Account of Christian Perfection as believed and taught by Mr. John Wesley from the year 1725 to the year 1777*. Seedbed Publishing. *The Path to Perfection: An Examination and Restatement of John Wesley's Doctrine of Christian Perfection*. W. E. Sangster, Epworth Press. *"Five Views on Sanctification"*. Dieter, Hoekema, Horton, McQuilkin, & Walvoord. Academic Books, Zondervan Publishing House. *Foundations of Wesleyan-Armininian Theology*. Mildred Bangs Wynkoop. *Charles Wesley on Sanctification: A Biographical and Theological Study*. John R. Tyson. Francis Asbury Press. *Holiness Reconsidered*. Paul F. Evans, Xulon Press. *Scriptural Holiness*. Noel Brooks, Advocate Press.

26   LSS. p. 69.

27   Ibid. p. 69. One must remember during Holmes childhood that he was trained in the *Shorter Westminster Catechism*. This catechism was influenced by the TULIP teachings of Calvinist theology. Holmes struggled with the new holiness teaching partly due to the teaching on Predestination. His struggles mirror the same issues as A. B. Simpson, the founder of the Christian and Missionary Alliance. Holmes and Simpson address the darkness cast over them by this teaching.

28   Ibid. p. 70.

29   Ibid. p. 71.

30   Ibid. pp. 71-72

31   Ibid. pp. 74-75. The bold and italics are emphasized by me. These insights are key to understanding the change from Holmes' youthful enthusiasm and carelessness to God shaping a vessel for His Work.

32   Ibid. p. 76.

33   Ibid. p. 79.

34   Ibid. pp. 81-82.

35   Ibid. p. 82.

36   Ibid. pp. 83-84.

37   Ibid,. p. 85.

38   Ibid. pp. 87-88.

39   Ibid. pp. 93-94.

40   *Old Time Power: A Centennial History of the International Pentecostal Holiness Church*. Vinson Synan. pp. 34-35. LifeSprings.

41   Ibid. p. 35.

42   *David M.Rubenstein Rare Book & Manuscript Library*, Duke University. Box 1.

43   *The Cincinnati Enquirer,* 9/9/1897, Volume LIV No. 232, No Page Number (NPN).

44   *The Louisville Courier-Journal, Louisville, KY.* 9.10/1897. NPN.

45   *The Louisville Courier-Journal,* 9/16,/1897.

46   *Burlingame Enterprise,* 12/23/1897. NPN.

47   *The Louisville Courier-Journal,* 12/24.1897. NPN.

48   Ibid,. pp. 97.

49   *Anderson Intelligencer,* Anderson, S. May 3, 1899, Volume XXIV—NO. 45. p.1. Referred to as AI.

50   Ibid. p.1.

51   Ibid. p.1.

52   *The Great Revival: Beginnings of the Bible Belt.* John B. Boles, pp. 150-151. Referred to as JB.

53   Ibid. p. 152.

54   Ibid. p. 153.

55   Ibid. p. 163.

56   Ibid. p. 164.

57   *A. B. Simpson: His Message and Impact on the Third Great Awakening."* Michael G. Yount, p. 39. Referred to as YGY.

58   Ibid. pp. 42-44.

59   *A History 1898-1915: Pentecostal Mission, Holiness Organized or Unorganized?* Trevecca Press, Nashville, TN. p. 88. Referred to as HPM.

60   Revised Standard Version of the Bible, copyright © 1946, 1952, and 1971 the Division of Christian Education of the National Council of the Churches of Christ in the United States of America. Underlines and bold print emphasis are mine.

61   Holmes Bible College Archives. Nina Holmes "The Holmes Bible and Missionary Institute". p. 1. N.D.

62   Nina Holmes history. p. 1.

63   Ibid. p. 93.

64   Ibid. p. 93.

65   Ibid. p. 94.

66   Ibid. p. 94.

67   David Rubenstein Library. Box 1.

68   Ella Brown would eventually marry George Floyd Taylor, the author of *The Spirit and The Bride*, the first doctrinal work on the Baptism of the Holy Spirit. The Taylors and Holmes became best friends. Rev. Holmes would conduct the 1905 graduation ceremonies at Bethel Holiness School in Rose Hill, North Carolina. Miss Brown was originally a member of the Pentecostal Free Will Baptist Church.

69   *The Altamont Witness*. June 22, 1914 p. 4. Later notes identified as LAW.

70   Ibid. June 22, 1914 p. 4.

71   Ibid. July 8, 1914 p. 3.

72   Ibid. July 8, 1914 p. 3.

73   LSS. p. 95-96.

74   Ibid. p 99.

75   Ibid. p. 101.

76   Ibid. p. 103.

77   *The Christian and Missionary Alliance*. n. d. p. 545. Later this publication identified as *TCAMA*. An interesting note is A. B. Crumpler held a Holiness Meeting in Magnolia, N.C. on May 14, 1897. Mattie Perry's father was one of the guest speakers. Also, another important note is that these meetings introduced George Floyd Taylor to the Holiness Movement and Sanctification. Plus, during these meetings, Taylor met his future wife, Ella Brown from Turkey, N.C. and one of the initial students at Altamont.

78   Ibid, February, 6 1898 p. 156.

79   Ibid. June 6, 1899 p. 29.

80   Ibid. June 10, 1898 p. 29.

81   Ibid. August 5, 1899 p. 157.

82   Ibid. September 9, 1899 p. 232.

83   Ibid. August 7, 1899 p. 76 and August 12, 1899 p. 172.

84   TAW. July 8, 1914 p. 3.

85   Ibid. July 8, 1914 p. 3.

86   Ibid. July 8, 1914 p. 4.

87   *TCAMA*. March 3, 1900 p. 160.

88   TWA. July 8, 1914 p. 4. The name change on this move includes Alliance. One may question, if the school move was related to Holmes, Todd, Pike, and

Houston attending the Southern Convention meetings in Atlanta and teaching the Four Fold Gospel of A. B. Simpson. When J. O. McClurkan begins to attend the Southern Convention, the Pentecostal Mission group sent prospective students to Nyack for ministerial studies. Keep in mind Holmes always established the Institute as non-denominational as did Simpson in leading the CMA.

89   An article is supported in *The Laurens Advertiser.* October 14, 1903, p. 3. *The State* newspaper from Columbia, South Carolina.carried an article of the Bible Institute move to Columbia, South Carolina on April 9, 1903, p.8.

90   LSS. p. 135. At the same time the Welsh Revival was covering Wales. This spirit of prayer reached around the world during

91   *A History of 1898-1915 Pentecostal Mission Incorporated.* Trevecca Press, Nashville. 1977. pp. 228, 231, & 234. Identified as HPM. Keep in mind Pike was a minister in the Methodist Episcopal South Church and manager of *The Way of Faith*, he published news for the Holiness Movement around the country. Later he will be challenged to end publishing of Azusa Street reports and other articles on the new Pentecostal outpouring.

92   LSS. p. 117. This statement appears to affirm Holmes' realization that Altamont was a chosen location to build his vision of a Bible School. There are no known existing letters or diaries by Holmes to reveal the depth of the school's previous moves to Atlanta or Columbia.

93   LSS. p. 118. TAW. August 8, 1914. p3 3. The move to Atlanta was the initial beginning of this faith move.

94   Ibid. p. 135.

95   *International Dictionary of Pentecostal Charismatic Movements Revised and Expanded.* Stanley M. Burgess, Editor and Eduard M. Van Der Maas, Associate Editor. Zondervan, Grand Rapids, Michigan, 2002. pp. 1017-1018. Identified as INDPCM.

96   Ibid. p. 1187.

97   *A. B. Simpson and The Pentecostal Movement: A Study in Continuity, Crisis, and Change.* Charles W. Nienkirchen. Wipf and Stock Publishers, 1992. p. 79. Identified as ABSATPM.

98   LSS. p. 135. Holmes was speaking of answered prayers during the 1905 prayer season.

99   Ibid. p. 136. Rev. J. M. Pike's relationship began in the 1890s as they ministered together in the CMA. Also, the school moved from Atlanta to Columbia, SC, the Olive Branch Mission became the new school location. The Olive Branch Mission was the site of publishing *The Way of Faith.*

100   Ibid. p. 136.

101   Ibid. p. 136.

102   Ibid. p. 137.

103   *Azusa East: The Life and Times of G. B. Cashwell* by Doug Beacham. *Fire in the Carolinas: The Revival Legacy of G. B. Cashwell and A. B. Crumpler* by Michael Thornton.

104   LSS. p. 137.

105   Ibid. p. 138.

106   Ibid. p. 139.

107   Ibid. p. 139.

108   Ibid. p. 141.

109   Ibid. p. 141.

110   King's concern for the Holy Spirit Baptism with evidence of tongues is well understood. He had been a member of the Fire Baptized Holiness movement under B.H. Irvin. Irvin taught the Baptism with fire and included other baptisms of Dynamite, Lyddite, and Oxidite. King later became the leader of the Fire Baptized and worked to correct this extraneous teachings of Irwin. *Fire Baptized: The Many Lives and Works of Benjamin Hardin Irwin: A Biography and a Reader.* by Vinson Synan and Daniel Woods.

111   LSS. pp. 141-142.

112   Ibid. pp. 144-145.

113   Ibid. p. 147.

114   Ibid. p. 147.

115   Ibid. p. 149. S.A. Bishop became a leader in The Pentecostal Holiness Church and leader of the Southern Pentecostal Association. He pastored the great church in Birmingham, Alabama.

116   Ibid. p. 88.

117   Ibid. p. 89.

118   *Exploring Christian Holiness: Volume 1 the Biblical Foundations.* W. T Purkiser, 1983. p. 120. Referred to ECH.

119   Ibid. p. 120.

120   HPM. p. 94.

121   LSS. p. 152-153.

122   Ibid. p. 153.

123   Ibid. p. 158.

124   Ibid. p. 159.

125   Ibid. p. 162.

126   The Daily Recorder. Columbia, S.C. June 18, 1908, p.1. Notice carefully the term 'families in Laurens' addresses N. J. Holmes and S. C. Todd. as unnamed supporters.

127   Ibid. p. 1.

128   LSS. pp. 162-163.

129   Ibid. p. 166.

130   Ibid. p. 166.

131   Ibid. p. 167.

132   Ibid. p. 170.

133   Ibid. p. 171.

134   Ibid. p. 172.

135   Ibid. p. 173.

136   Ibid. p. 178.

137   Ibid. p. 178-179.

138   The Advocate Holiness, G. F. Taylor, January 20, 1920. Vol. 3 No. 43. "Nickels John Holmes". pp. 3-5.

139   Ibid. p. 240.

140   TAW. p. 1.

141   LSS. p. 244.

142   Ibid. p. 247.

143   Ibid. p. 249. It must be remembered Taylor held the Commencement Exercises at Altamont in 1907 at which the school experienced the Pentecostal Outpouring with evidence of tongues speaking. Holmes and Taylor maintained a blessed relationship until Holmes passing. Taylor served as a preacher for the camp meetings for Rev. Holmes.

144   Ibid. p. 252.

145   Ibid. p. 252.

146   PHA, 'Nickels John Holmes" p. 3.

147   Ibid. p. 253.

148   Discovery by Rev. Zachary Tomlinson in Joel Sexton's *History of the Upper*

South Carolina Conference.

149   PHA. p. 4.

150   Ibid. p. 256.

151   Ibid. p. 265.

152   Ibid. p. 269.

153   PHA. p. 5.

154   Mrs. Iva Thomas, *The History of Holmes Theological Seminary.* n. d. p. 25. Identified as HHTS.

155   TVH. February 1969. p. 3.

156   Ibid. pp. 27-32.

157   The Holmes Bulletin: New for the Institute Family and Friends. April 1942. p. 1. Identified as THB.

158   Ibid. p. 2.

159   Ibid. p. 3.

160   HHTS. p. 3.

161   The Voice of Holmes. January 1947. p. 5. Identified as TVH. . HHTS, pp. 32-33.

162   TVH. p. 6.

163   TVH. April 1947. p, 6.

164   TVH. November 1947. pp. 2-9.

165   HHTS. p. 37.

166   Unknown publication. p. 5. In the Holmes Bible College Archives Department.

167   Unknown publication. pp. 5-6.

168   Legacy. com. Dr. Kenneth D. Benson. pp. 1-2.

169   Unknown publication. n.d.. no page number.

170   Unknown publication. n. d. no page number.

171   Holmes Magazine. Winter 1998. pp. 2, 4-5. Identified as HM.

172   Ibid. pp. 1-5.

173   HM. May 2000. pp. 1, 8.

174   HM. Summer 2001. p. 2.

175   HM. Winter 2002. pp. 1-3, 8.

176   HM. Fall 2004. pp. 1-2.

177   Hugh's News & Commentary. Dr. G. Earl Beatty named Interim President of Holmes Bible College. pp. 4-6.

178   Hugh's News & Commentary. President Leggett Honored Upon Retirement. March 29, 2017.

179   The Co-Worker. Miss Nina. October 1956.

180   Mrs. Iva Thomas, *The History of Holmes Theological Seminary*. n. d. p. 25. Identified as HHTS.

181   TVH. February 1969. p. 3.

182   Ibid. pp. 27-32.

183   The Holmes Bulletin: New for the Institute Family and Friends. April 1942. p. 1. Identified as THB.

184   Ibid. p. 2.

185   Ibid. p. 3.

186   HHTS. p. 3.

187   The Voice of Holmes. January 1947. p. 5. Identified as TVH. . HHTS, pp. 32-33.

188   TVH. p. 6.

189   TVH. April 1947. p, 6.

190   TVH. November 1947. pp. 2-9.

191   HHTS. p. 37.

192   Unknown publication. p. 5. In the Holmes Bible College Archives Department.

193   Unknown publication. pp. 5-6.

194   Legacy. com. Dr. Kenneth D. Benson. pp. 1-2.

195   Unknown publication. n.d.. no page number.

196   Unknown publication. n. d. no page number.

197   Holmes Magazine. Winter 1998. pp. 2, 4-5. Identified as HM.

198   Ibid. pp. 1-5.

199   HM. May 2000. pp. 1, 8.

200   HM. Summer 2001. p. 2.

201   HM. Winter 2002. pp. 1-3, 8.

202   HM. Fall 2004. pp. 1-2.

203   Hugh's News & Commentary. Dr. G. Earl Beatty named Interim President of Holmes Bible College. pp. 4-6.

204   Hugh's News & Commentary. President Leggett Honored Upon Retirement. March 29, 2017.

205   The Co-Worker. Miss Nina. October 1956.

About the Author

Stan York lives in Charlotte, North Carolina, and is married to Valerie Goode York. They have six children and six grandchildren. He attends Stanley Pentecostal Holiness Church and is ordained as a pastor in the IPHC Cornerstone Conference. Stan currently serves as the Director of the Cornerstone Archives. He earned a B.A. in History from East Carolina University, a Master of Divinity (1989) from Asbury Theological Seminary, a Master of Theology (1997) from Duke Divinity School, and a Ph. D. from Regent University (2012). Stan was a student of the late Dr. Vinson Synan. His dissertation is titled, *George Floyd Taylor: The Life of an Early Southern Pentecostal*. He wrote the *Centennial History of the Cornerstone Conference*. Stan also wrote a chapter on the Holiness/Pentecostal Denominational Development in North Carolina in *Religious Traditions of North Carolina: Histories, Tenets, and Leaders*: Editor W. Glenn Jonas, Jr. Stan has taught ministry classes for Zion Assembly of God in Cleveland and the IPHC History and the History of Christianity for the Biblical Ministries Institute for the Cornerstone Conference.